Defending the

Good Society

Defending the

Good Society

The Assault on Order, Justice, and Freedom

Larry G. Johnson

Copyright © 2020 by Larry G. Johnson.
All rights reserved.

Published by Anvil House Publishers, LLC Owasso, Oklahoma
www.anvilhousebooks.com

Printed in the United States of America.
Cover: Whitley Graphics

The website addresses recommended throughout this book are offered as a resource to you. Except for the articles posted by the author on culturewarrior.net, these websites are not intended in any way to be or imply an endorsement on the part of Larry G. Johnson or Anvil House Publishers, nor do we vouch for their content.

Scripture quotations marked KJV are taken from the Holy Bible, King James Version. Scripture quotations taken from the New King James Version. Copyright © 1979, 1980, 1982 by Thomas Nelson, Inc. Used by permission. All rights reserved.

ISBN: 978-0-9839716-7-2

Library of Congress Control Number: 2020915604

In honor and appreciation of our parents –
Members of the Greatest Generation

Glenn M. Johnson   Muriel Louise (Hart) Johnson
(1922-1984)   (1925-2004)

Merrill K. Kramer   Margaret Mae (McIntosh) Kramer
(1925-1980)   (1928-   )

Contents

Preface.. vi

Acknowledgements... ix

Defending the Good Society – The Assault on Order, Justice, and Freedom

Introduction... 1

Part I – Equality and the Good Society

1   Order, Worldview, Equality, and Egalitarianism........ 7

2   A Brief History of Equality............................... 15

3   Order and the Good Society.............................. 21

4   Justice and the Good Society............................. 27

5   Freedom and the Good Society........................... 31

Part II – Equality and Human Relationships

6   Equality and the God-Man Relationship................. 37

7   Equality and Marriage-Family Relationships............ 49

8   Equality and the Church-State Relationship............ 59

9   Equality and Man-Community Relationships........... 69

10   Equality and Labor-Property Relationships............. 79

11   Equality – Traditional v. Progressive Education...... 93

Contents

Part III – The Goddess of Equality and the Destruction of the Good Society

12	Assault on Language and Free Speech................	105
13	Erosion of the Principles of American Civil Order	115
14	The Spiraling Decline of American Moral Order...	123

Part IV – Defending and Preserving the Good Society

15	Defending the Good Society – A Time for Action by Faithful Christians..................................	133
16	The Good Society and the Organized Church......	139
17	The Faithful Remnant must follow the Narrow Path...	143

Addendum

	(1) Differences between Christian and Humanist Worldviews – a Summary.......................	149
	(2) Humanist definition of words used to dislodge the Judeo-Christian worldview from the central cultural vision of American – a Summary...........	154

Notes..	163
Selected Bibliography...	175
Index..	181

Preface

Two thousand years ago an itinerate preacher and a small band of his disciples trod the hills and valleys of ancient Palestine, a backwater province of the Roman Empire. This Jewish man was somewhat unique in that he claimed to be the Son of God sent to earth to testify to the truth and die on a cross for the sins of mankind. This did not please the local Jewish religious leaders who vehemently denied his deity and sought to end the threat to their authority. Eventually, they had him arrested and sent to Pontius Pilate, the Roman governor of the region. Pilate quizzed the preacher and said to Him, "Are You a king then?" Jesus answered, "You say *rightly* that I am a king. For this cause I was born, and for this cause I have come into the world, that I should bear witness to the truth. Everyone who is of the truth hears My voice." The governor did not look kindly upon the unrest created or potential threats to Roman authority by this preacher who claimed to be a king. Therefore, he had him crucified. End of problem and end of story. Or so they thought.

On Sunday morning following his crucifixion on Friday, Jesus rose from the dead and departed from the tomb in which he had been laid. He rallied his forlorn disciples and eventually was seen by five hundred people following his resurrection. For forty days before his ascension to his father in heaven, he taught his disciples and commissioned his followers to share the good news with the entire world. The Divinely inspired writings of both the Old and New Testaments were the foundations of a moral order to which His followers were to be guided through the centuries.

In spite of persecution, government sanctions, and the machinations of a misguided, compromised, corrupt, lukewarm, and even dead leadership in the organized church of that day, Christianity and its moral order spread throughout the world with remarkable success. But Christianity's greatest success in spreading the gospel came in the 1600s and 1700s with the joining of Christian moral order with a civil order built on biblical foundations which allowed the creation of the good society in America and eventually lifted England out of its moral and civic disorder.

The beginnings of the good society occurred in America in the early 1600s. Just before arriving on the shores of a vast wilderness that was America in 1620, the Pilgrims had solemnly and mutually pledged in the presence of God and each other to a "civil Body politick" under "just and equal laws...[for the] furtherance of the glory of God." Thus we have the beginnings of a good society. Within ten years and all through the following decade, a vast wave of Puritans began crossing the Atlantic for religious liberty. They sought reforms to bring about "a pure and stainless church." Sherwood Eddy called those early years of colonial Puritanism "...the finest expression of spiritual life that Britain or America or Continental Europe had at that time."[*] Although a work of trial and error in the beginning, it would eventually lead to the Constitution of the newly formed United States of America. Other separatist Christians of a like mind were left behind in England and would work toward the formation of a Christian moral and civic order throughout England and the British Empire.

Spurred by three great spiritual awakenings in America and England over the course of a century and a half beginning in the early 1720s, the good society produced an astonishing degree of order, justice, and freedom that had never been known in any civil order in the history of the world.

As America neared the end of the 1800s, there arose within society and portions of the church dangerous enemies of the good society that would challenge its moral and civic order. The success of the pervasive attacks on all facets of American life by its enemies has eroded, especially in the last seventy-five years, the order, justice, and freedom that the citizenry has enjoyed for most of two hundred and fifty years since America's founding.

The purpose of this book is to introduce the good society to many who are living today but have never been taught its origins, nature, and importance in maintaining order, justice, and freedom. The second purpose is to identify and expose the enemies of the good society and its foundations, the falseness of the enemy's ideologies, the strategies and tactics of their assault, and the inevitable demise of order, justice, and freedom should they be successful in destroying the good society. The third purpose is to give guidance to and prepare faithful Christians and their allies in defending the good society. The fourth and last purpose of this book is to encourage the faithful with the knowledge that ultimate victory belongs to Christ and His followers, either in this life or in the perfect society which is eternity with God hereafter.

―――――

Defending the Good Society represents a summation of much of what the author has written in his other books and articles, subjects he has taught, and a lifetime of reading, study, and thought with regard to these matters. Small portions of the author's other books and writings have been integrated into or modified for use in this book, especially *Ye shall be as gods – Humanism and Christianity – The Battle for*

---

[*] Sherwood Eddy, *The Kingdom of God and the American Dream*, (New York: Harper & Brothers Publishers, 1941), pp. 48, 56.

Supremacy in the American Cultural Vision. Also, portions of various articles posted on the author's website *CultureWarrior.net* also have been integrated into or modified for use in this book. With some exceptions, the use of the author's other writings are not annotated herein.

Acknowledgements

Most acknowledgments by the authors of books speak of those individuals who were closely helpful to the author in accomplishing his project, some more than others. This is right and proper. In this vain, I want to acknowledge the invaluable help of my Sherryl, my wife and love of almost a half century. Without her constant insights, suggestions, editing, and encouragement, this book would have been far less than it is and perhaps would not have been written.

Apart from those who directly assisted and influenced the writing of a book, there is another group that authors often overlook in their acknowledgments, those of past generations that made possible the prosperity and freedoms which afforded writers the opportunity to apply their craft. Since this book is about defending the good society, we must acknowledge those generations in America and England that built and sustained societies founded upon a moral and civil order that made possible the highest degree of order, justice, and freedom of any society in the history of the world.

Who were the people that built those good societies where much of world's population desire to go to and live? I have searched for words to describe them but kept coming back to the words I wrote in 2008 in the Acknowledgements section of in my first book, *Tar Creek – A History of the Quapaw Indians, the World's Largest Lead and Zinc Discovery, and the Tar Creek Superfund Site*. I was writing about many different peoples who converged on a small area in far northeastern Oklahoma over many generations. But on a larger scale, that description really fits all generations of Americans since the Pilgrims landed on its shore in 1620. For just a moment let us look back at this people, their history, and their culture that modern-day humanists, leftists, progressives, socialists, anarchists, and other ideologues want to cancel.

> I could not help feeling a tremendous admiration for this people... these ordinary Americans. No pretense was made to be what they were not. They and millions like them scattered across the continent and made America great. They fought its wars, built its cities, and made a civil society civil, and then looked beyond their own backyard to help others around the world. Most aren't off to protest the latest perceived wrong, save the most recent endangered species, claim victim status over some slight, or be consumed with the latest pop-culture or tragedy-comedy emanating from Hollywood. People often mock their values and call them ignorant and out-

of-touch. They aren't perfect and wouldn't pretend to be if they knew how. When life hits them with a fast curve ball, they grimace but carry the pain silently, and then take their base. They take their turn, say "please" and "thank you," and salute the flag. They can't help it. It's in their DNA.

They are generally pitied by the intellectuals, government officials, and far-off social-planners that wish to control their lives as opposed to making it possible for them to plan their own lives. To some, these people often become the fodder for their latest version of Farm-aid, some other do-good project, or other celebrity cause with which to consume the time of their own meaningless lives. What these ordinary Americans do is work hard, hold their families together and provide for them as best as they can, respect authority, love God, and protect their country. They are a tough race of survivors that brought us through the perilous twentieth century including the Great Depression, four major wars, and the cold war. In this hour of the self-absorbed, self-indulgent "me" generation, they and others like them are becoming anachronisms. That is the real internal threat to America.*

We are now living in an age where those whose words, ideas, and actions that support the good society are not tolerated. The good society is under a full-scale attack which has been popularly called Cancel Culture. This attack is not subtle but a blatant frontal attack on the values, history, and culture of Western civilization and in particular the good society described in this book. But we must be up to the challenge. If we wish to acknowledge and honor those past generations of Americans, we must join the battle and defend the good society.

Larry G. Johnson - Owasso, Oklahoma
September 30, 2020

---

* Larry G. Johnson, *Tar Creek – A History of the Quapaw Indians, the World's Largest Lead and Zinc Discovery, and the Tar Creek Superfund Site*, (Owasso, Oklahoma: Anvil House Publishing, 2008), pp. 8-9.

Books by Larry G. Johnson

Tar Creek – A History of the Quapaw Indians, the World's Largest Lead and Zinc Discovery, and the Tar Creek Superfund Site. ©2008 [Finalist - Oklahoma Book Award Non-fiction Book of the Year 2010 by the Oklahoma Center for the Book, the state affiliate of the Center for the Book at the Library of Congress.]

Ye shall be as gods – Humanism and Christianity – The Battle for Supremacy in the American Cultural Vision. ©2011 (Study Guide available: Student and Teacher Editions)

Evangelical Winter – Restoring New Testament Christianity. ©2016

Culture Wars – Dispatches from the Front. ©2016

True Revival – Reviving the Church in Every Generation. ©2018

Defending the Good Society – The Assault on Order, Justice, and Freedom. ©2020

Defending the Good Society – The Assault on Order, Justice, and Freedom

Introduction

Throughout the history of mankind there has been a worldwide and perpetual war between good and evil. This war did not begin with the creation of mankind but reaches back beyond time into the heavenlies when an arrogant pride arose in the bosom of the angel Satan. His beauty and exalted position assigned to him by God led him to elevate himself to being the equal of God, his creator. As a result of Satan's rebellion, he was not only demoted and stripped of every precious stone that was his covering, he was cast out of heaven but not before he deceived a third of the angels who were also cast out.

So Satan really hates God. It is a vicious, snarling, consuming hatred—something almost beyond the ability of humans to comprehend. But Satan had no power to directly strike back at God. His only alternative was to strike at God by robbing the Creator of His relationship with man—His special creation. Satan's rebellion and that of man is called sin, and sin will ultimately destroy the thing for which man was created—a loving, eternal relationship with God.

Man was created with God's divine image stamped upon him. This likeness was not in the physical sense but spiritual. Human beings are unique among all of God's creations because each has both a material body and an immaterial soul/spirit. Having an image or likeness of God (imago dei) means that man was made to resemble God. There are three facets of this likeness. *Mentally*, we are like God because man is a volitional, rational agent who can reason and choose. *Morally*, we are like God in that man was created in righteousness and perfect innocence which reflects God's holiness. *Socially*, man humanity was created for fellowship with God and his fellowman which reflects God's triune nature and His love.

Having been created in God's likeness, it was necessary for man to have freewill in order for a mutually loving relationship to exist. God did not create man out of need. Rather, it was a will to love, an expression of the very character of God, to share the inner life of the Trinity. By creating man with a free will meant the possibility of man's rejection of God and His love. Being God, He knew the course and cost of His creation would be the death of His Son on the cross to make possible a means for man to re-establish his relationship with God. In other words, freewill and the potential for rejection of God was the penalty for the possibility of love. So it is on the earthly plane, to risk love is to risk rejection. Love is a choice because man has freewill, and true love reflects the divine in that it *focuses on relationships and not self*.

Here we begin to see the perpetual war between good and evil can be more precisely defined as being a battle between those who are God-centered versus those who are man-centered. In the battle of worldviews in the Western world, it is the battle between the *God's relationship-centered biblical worldview* and man's *self-centered humanistic worldview*.

Man's freewill became the primary tool used by Satan to attack and destroy man's relationship with God. Now we begin to see the fundamental difference between Christianity and humanism that shapes the differences between those worldviews and how each defines freedom. In the Christian worldview, *freedom simply means a lack of coercion but also implies self-restraint and deference to relational patterns* revealed in the mores, norms, tradition, and distant voices of the past. True freedom is found only when an individual chooses a right relationship with God through the acceptance of Christ as his or her Lord and Savior. By right relationship we mean a relationship unbroken by sin and rebellion. In a right relationship with God, man chooses to subordinate his own freewill to Christ's, to accept Him, and to follow the road of freedom found in the revelation to the ancient Hebrews and first century Christians. From this foundation of a right relationship with God, man can find right relationships with his fellowman in family, community, and state which make the good society possible.

In the contrary view of *freedom that exalts self*, humanists attempt to *release the individual from the relational patterns* flowing from those same mores, norms, mores and traditions, and distant voices of the past. Man is centered on self and a pawn of his senses. However, the destruction of a society's divinely ordered relational patterns by the god of self results in loneliness, pain, suffering, and loss in this life and eternity thereafter.

In other words, true freedom is found in freely subduing one's will to that of God's will as opposed to the false freedom sought through the exaltation of self and deference to one's sensual nature. Christ's words in Luke's gospel capture the essence of the seeming enigma of freewill.

> Then He said to *them* all, "If anyone desires to come after Me, let him deny himself, and take up his cross daily, and follow Me. For whoever desires to save his life will lose it, but whoever loses his life for My sake will save it." [Luke 9: 23-24. NKJV]

Satan and humanism's opposition to God's plan for mankind encompasses all of human history. The humanistic spirit of the world is of satanic origin and has been present within human society since Adam and Eve were driven from the Garden. All through history, this humanistic spirit of the world is the *spirit of rebellion* of man against God. It is the essence of Original Sin that infects all humanity.

Part I – Equality and the Good Society

The good society is inhabited by a people who have constructed and maintain a high degree of moral and social order founded upon and held together by the glue of eternal truths, norms, human universals, mores and traditions, distant voices of the past, and most importantly faithfulness to God and the prescriptions of the Bible. In such a society will be found a high degree of *order, justice, and freedom.*

It is at this point that many non-Christians who approve of and value the attributes and provisions of the good society will reject the God of the Bible as the fountain of truth from which the good society must draw its pattern and sustenance. But that cannot be as will be shown throughout this book. Any source other than God's perfect truth as shown in His creation and revelation to the ancient Israelites and first century Christians is less than perfect. Over the course of time, that source will be revealed as flawed and inevitably lead to disorder and disintegration of any society based on imperfect truth. I ask that that the skeptic continue reading and reserve judgment on this point until the end of the book.

This book's hypothesis is that the ongoing efforts to destroy the good society are a consequence of *applied* humanism as it is imposed on the everyday life of Americans in the grip of *forced* equality. The dominant humanistic concept of forced equality is disintegrative because of its nature and presents not only a false philosophy and view of the world but is doing significant if not fatal damage to American society and the world. From these premises and perspective, the author has titled this book *Defending the Good Society – The Assault on Order, Justice, and Freedom.*

1

Order, Worldview, Equality, and Egalitarianism

This book examines one facet of the conflict between the truth of Christianity's belief in the Judeo-Christian God and the lie of humanism's man-centric interpretations of existence. That facet upon which we will focus is humanism's imposition on the good society of radical egalitarianism's flawed doctrines of equality. Along the way in the examination of radical egalitarianism, the rotten heart of hydra-headed humanism and its many tentacles will be examined and exposed.

Archimedes once said, "Give me a place to stand, and a lever long enough, and I will move the world."[1] Egalitarianism is just one of humanism's multifaceted attacks on truth which is being used to destroy and replace the good society, but over the last three hundred years egalitarianism has become humanism's lever used to tilt the world toward a humanistic view of life which denies God. But these efforts are doomed to failure because both egalitarianism's lever and fulcrum are constructed of the humanistic spirit of the world and its false philosophies. The false philosophies fail because they are incapable of producing a good society which must align with the truth of the image of God qualities imprinted on the nature of mankind. From the failure of humanism's lever of egalitarianism, we shall expose the entirety of humanism's disordering and disintegrative concepts throughout society.

Order

Before we examine modern concepts of equality and its impact on society and the various facets of its culture, we must understand what societies are and how they develop, operate, and evolve through time. There are universal components necessary for the long-term survival of the good society, and that survival depends on the degree to which three essential components are integrated and guarded in that culture. Therefore, we must examine the interdependent nature of those components and how an attack on one endangers the others and threatens culture.

Russell Kirk identified the three universal components of the good society: *order, justice, and freedom*.

> Order is the first need of the *soul*. It is not possible to love what one ought to love, unless we recognize some principles of order by which to govern ourselves.

> Order is the first need of *commonwealth*. It is not possible for us to live in peace with one another, unless we recognize some principle of order by which to do justice.
>
> The good society is marked by a high degree of *order, justice, and freedom*. Among these, order has primacy: for justice cannot be enforced until a tolerable civil social order is attained, nor can freedom be anything better than violence until order gives us laws.[2] [emphasis added]

The converse of the good society is the bad society, and by inference it is a society characterized by disorder, injustice, and bondage. Most societies are found somewhere on the spectrum between the polar opposites of the good and bad societies. For example, some societies may have a high degree of civil order but lack moral order. Such order is downwardly imposed by a select few rather than an order chosen and established by the citizenry. This order imposed by the few occurs at the expense of justice and freedom of the members of that society. Such an imposed order creates injustice and bondage of that society's inmates.

It is only when we have a proper, working understanding of the three universal components of a good society that one can examine concepts such as equality and its long-term impact on a society's order, justice, and freedom—either for good or ill.

It is important for the reader to remember that when we speak of *order* throughout this book as being the first of the three universal components of a good society, we mean an *order* that includes both the order of the soul and order of society (*moral* order and *civic* order). Moral order and social order are complementary, intricately linked, and interdependent. Disorder of one leads to disorder of the other.[3] However, in some sections of this book we shall examine moral order and civic order individually with respect to various aspects of the good society, humanism, equality, and other concepts.

Worldview and the Search for Truth

The war between good and evil may be defined as being a war between two competing worldviews. Therefore, we must understand the meaning of the term "worldview" and how they develop over time in individuals and societies as a whole.

Richard Weaver's *Visions of Order* is one of the most articulate descriptions of the formation and preservation of an enduring culture.

> As far as one can tell, the collective consciousness of the group creates a mode of looking at the world or arrives at some imaginative visual bearing. It "sees" the world metaphorically according to some felt need of the group, and this entails an ordering which denotes dissatisfaction with "things as they are."…It is of the essence of culture to feel its own imperative and to believe in the uniqueness of its worth…Culture derives its very desire to continue from its unitariness…There is at the heart of every culture a center of authority from which there proceed subtle and pervasive pressures upon us to conform and to repel the unlike as disruptive…it must insist on a pattern of inclusion and exclusion.[4]

Cultures may be said to be similar to a mirror in that it is reflective of its citizens' collective consciousness. However, the cultural mirror not only reflects society but at the same time informs society of its necessities, obligations, constraints, and worth which provide subtle and pervasive pressures to support and defend the culture being reflected.

When a culture loses its cohesiveness, exclusivity, or center of authority, it loses the ability to inform its citizens and places the culture on the road to disorder and ultimate disintegration. Such a culture, using our analogy of the cultural mirror, becomes distorted and similar to those found in a carnival funhouse. The culture can no longer adequately reflect the worldviews once held by its citizens and slides into disunity as it becomes a "…democratic culture…open to everybody at all times on equal terms."[5] However, the emerging egalitarian culture may not immediately replace the former dying culture but merely places it in hospice until its eventual death.

The new cultural masters of the egalitarian society do not treat the source of rampant disorder but merely the symptoms with an ever expanding array of humanistic tonics and poultices in an attempt to make life tolerable for the inmates.

Apart from all that has been said about the elements necessary for a culture to survive and thrive, those elements in and of themselves do not insure survival. In addition to a culture's unity or cohesiveness, the belief in its uniqueness and worth, and its insistence on a pattern of inclusion and exclusion, the collective consciousness of citizens that form the culture *must align with truth,* and by truth is meant *objective truth.* If a culture is based on a false worldview that does not adequately answer the basic questions of life, that culture will also decline and eventually die.

As we have noted, cultures do not unilaterally develop worldviews but are reflective of the collective worldviews of its citizens. Thus, building a worldview begins with the individual. To determine how individuals develop their respective worldviews, we begin with a question: What is the most pondered subject in all of mankind's history? Is it how to end all wars or eliminate hunger, sickness, suffering, or achieve other praiseworthy goals? Although these worthy endeavors and much else is on the mind of modern man, these questions are not of universal concern for all people in all societies for all time. But, there is still one question that consumes every human on the planet. Yet, the vast majority of people are not aware of this nagging question which they consciously or unconsciously seek to answer every day of their existence. That question is: What is truth? Some people often phrase the question another way: What is the meaning of life? But even this restatement is too narrow for it assumes that life as we understand it is all there is, and it does not answer how this life fits into the larger scheme of things and, for some, if there is a larger scheme of things.

By now the reader may be scratching his or her head and puzzling over the author's claim that every human being is concerned with discovering truth every day of their lives. The reader may have doubts about the assertion and wonders what the discovery of truth has to do with his or her daily life of work, family, health, debts, and all of the other challenges consuming one's waking hours each and every day. He or she may argue that they have no time for philosophical discussions and debates, especially when it doesn't get the bills paid, kids raised, and life lived. But I ask our puzzled reader to stay with me for a moment longer.

The heart of the difficulty in determining what is truth begins with the perspective from which we search for it. And that perspective may be described as our worldview, and like a naval, we all have one. And not only do we have a worldview, we are continually refining and updating it every day of our lives. That refining process is called a search for truth or as we have framed the question: What is truth?" This search involves both the daily minutiae of living as well as the basic questions of life such as who are we and where did we come from, how did we get in the mess we are in, and how do we get out of it? Now in this daily refining process we do not start afresh every day. Once truths have proven themselves incontrovertible, we build upon those and test new ideas, thoughts, experiences, and concepts in light of that which has proven true in the past. As we slowly build our worldview we find that it must be coherent and consistent, that is, we cannot comfortably hold beliefs that are in conflict or diametrically opposed.

In Western cultures the search for truth is dominated by two general perspectives, and these worldviews are battling for supremacy in every aspect of life. One is the Judeo-Christian worldview and its view of objective truth which the Founders held and which was the basis for the central cultural vision of America's first 150 years. The other worldview is humanism, rapidly ascending in American culture for the last one hundred years. In the last fifty years it has substantially captured the institutions of American life, most of its leadership, and a large percentage of its citizens. Humanism denies the supernatural and says, like Paul Kurtz, that truth is merely "...the product of the free give and take of conflicting opinions."[6] In other words, truth is simply what we perceive it to be. From a biblically-based worldview I would challenge the assumption that truth is determined by our individual perceptions and declare that truth is objectively determined and derived from our understanding of God and His nature as revealed in His creation and the biblical record.

Do these fundamental differences between the two worldviews leave us at a stalemate in our search for truth? How do we determine who's view of truth is right? There is a story told about Plato by an ancient commentator that, *on the surface*, appears to confirm the notion that our search for truth may be futile.

> Shortly before his death, Plato had a dream that he was a swan flitting from tree to tree and eluding the bird-catchers. When Simmias the Socratic heard this, he interpreted it to mean that all men would try to grasp Plato's meaning but that *none would succeed, and each would interpret him according to their own views.*[7] [emphasis added]

Must we agree with the ancient commentator that the stalemate between truth and opinion can never be broken? The answer is an unequivocal *No!* The ancient commentator was wrong. *We can know truth.* To know truth we must begin by examining the elements of a worldview and the reasons we must be concerned about it.

Worldview "...is a comprehensive framework of one's basic *beliefs* about *things*." Things include the world, human life, social morality, education, family, and God. Beliefs are not just innocuous feelings, opinions, or hypotheses. Beliefs are claims to a certain kind of knowledge one is willing to defend, that is, those beliefs to which one is committed. In other words, beliefs have to do with one's convictions. Lastly, worldview deals with *basic* beliefs about things—ultimate questions with which we are confronted, matters of general principle.[8]

Why must we concern ourselves with worldview? We are concerned because a worldview is concerned with the search for truth which is exceptionally important for one's survival in the jungle of life. The beliefs one hold tends to create a pattern, design, or structure that fit together in a particular way. This structure or order generally has a coherence or consistency; although, some inconsistencies may exist within one's worldview. This coherence, consistency, or order within one's worldview gives orientation and direction for living life. If a person's actions and beliefs are not consistent, the conflict must be resolved or over a period of time or a person's integrity and mental health will be diminished.[9] Therefore, a person must discover what is true and live a life compatible with that truth.

Here we have a clue to breaking the stalemate between conflicting worldviews and discovering the meaning of truth in spite of the ancient commentator's sentiment that meaning can only arise to the level of one's perspective and no more. To break this stalemate, we must examine the conflicting worldviews to determine which one is most *coherent, consistent with one's observation and experience, and gives orientation and direction for living life,* that is, which worldview reflects reality.

Equality and Egalitarianism

And it is this approach we must use when examining the concept of equality and the truth or falsity of its modern definitions, applications, and impact on the various institutions of American life: religion, government, the family, education, science (physical, biological, and social), economics and business, and popular culture. Where a worldview fails to reflect reality, we must expose that failure and redirect culture. Where it succeeds, we must embrace and promote it. It is within the scope of this book to make that examination.

In summary, our understanding of equality and its place and role in American culture will be a product of our worldview. The reader should know the worldview of the author during our journey to understanding equality. The author holds a biblical worldview which embraces objective truth with regard to the concept of equality, its operation, and status in society.

The subject of equality has become a central and dominating concept in almost every aspect of American life. We will examine many opinions, beliefs, concepts, and claims presented by a multitude of people, both living and dead. We will examine the concept of equality in history and as debated in today's latest newspaper, magazine, talk show, and Internet blog or podcast. This examination of the modern concept of equality is *not meant to be an academic exercise* but a practical primer concerned with how we live today as well as a blueprint to shape the culture that our children and grandchildren will inherit. The book is meant to engage every adult in an examination of the concept of equality whether the reader is a stay-at-home mom or a corporate executive, a twenty-something or an octogenarian. This examination of equality and how citizens engage and refine the concept is exceptionally important because how society views equality will determine how we live life in the remainder of the twenty-first century.

We have described the Good Society and now we must define its nemesis—humanism and its tool of egalitarianism.

- *Humanism* - a philosophy that is opposed to all forms of mythological illusions (religious or ideological) about man and his place in the universe. This means that Humanism involves some scientific view of nature and of man. Any theistic interpretation of the universe and any eschatological drama about divine beginnings and ends are rejected because it is logically meaningless and empirically unverified.[10]

- *Egalitarianism* - a belief in human equality especially with respect to social, political, and economic affairs; a social philosophy advocating the removal of inequalities among people.[11] Synonyms: doctrine, school of thought, philosophical system.

- *Equality* - the quality or state of being equal.[12] Synonyms: equivalency, par, parity, sameness.

- *Equity* - justice according to natural law or right specifically, freedom from bias or favoritism.[13] Synonyms: evenhandedness, fair-mindedness, fairness, impartiality, justice, objectiveness.

It is obvious that the definitions of equality and egalitarianism are not the same. Equality is merely recognition of equal portions residing in two or more entities. However, the true definition of equality does not pretend authority to assign worth or significance to the components measured.

Egalitarianism on the other hand is a philosophical system that attempts to recognize, establish, or assign equalities based on its doctrines and ideals. Having no legitimate authority, egalitarianism has presumed to impose its doctrines and school of thought in the affairs of men when dealing with values, standards, morals, ethics beliefs, principles, and worth.

In an attempt to legitimize its over-reach, egalitarianism has appropriated the words "equal, just, and fair" as being synonymous for its root word "egalitarian." When egalitarianism wrongly applies the meaning of "equality, justice, and fairness" to itself, they become little more than fleeting, ill-defined, and inappropriate euphemisms. As egalitarianism is radicalized, the words "equal, just, and fair" become the opposites of the very things egalitarianism claims to be. Those synonyms rightly belong to "equity" which is the quality of being fair or impartial and to which egalitarianism cannot lay claim.

Unfortunately, we live in an age where a large majority of people seem to have lost their ability to think critically. This loss of critical analysis has also diminished their ability to distinguish differences in the fundamental meaning of words. Whether by way of ignorant, numb, or lazy minds, the meanings of egalitarianism, equality, and equity have come to mean the same thing. Having blurred the distinctions, egalitarianism's elites have self-commissioned themselves to be the arbiters of equality, justice, and fairness in all matters with respect to the social, political, and economic affairs of society. Thus, *for purposes of this book* we shall use humanism's new definition of equality to mean egalitarianism and use these two terms interchangeably. As noted at the beginning of this chapter, egalitarianism's equality is humanism's lever to tilt the world towards its worldview and away from the Judeo-Christian worldview.

2

A Brief History of Equality

Right understanding of Equality requires a right understanding of Truth

As previously stated, our understanding of equality depends on our worldview or conception of truth. We need merely to examine history to understand that the quest for truth is a universal quest and covers all of man's history. Confucius living in the 6th and 5th centuries B.C. said, "The aim of a superior man is truth."[14] Confucius' value of truth was echoed by Plato, "The truth is the beginning of every good thing, both in heaven and on earth; and he who would be blessed and happy should be from the first a partaker of truth, for then he can be trusted."[15]

Almost four centuries later in another small country on the eastern rim of the Mediterranean, a dialogue was being held with regard to truth. Jesus had been delivered by Caiaphas, the Jewish high priest, to the front of the judgment hall in Jerusalem for judgment by the Roman governor. Asked by Pilate if he was a king, Jesus replied, "…'You say rightly that I am a king. For this cause I was born, and for this cause I have come into the world, that I should bear witness to the truth. Everyone who is of the truth hears My voice.' Pilate said to Him, '*What is truth?*' And when he had said this, he went out again to the Jews, and said to them, 'I find no fault in Him at all.'" [John 18:37-38. NKJV] [emphasis added]

Although truth has been highly valued through the millennia, beginning with the late 17th century and throughout the 18th century, new suspicions and slanders regarding the meaning of truth arose from the age of Enlightenment. According to T. H. Huxley, "It is the customary fate of new truths to begin as heresies and to end as superstitions."[16] By the 20th century, the historical meaning of truth had been robbed of its objectivity. Humanist Paul Kurtz wholly redefined the meaning of truth when he said, "…truth is often the product of the free give and take of conflicting opinions."[17]

Humanism's equality and the perversion of Truth

Man's quest for equality and its attendant appeals to pride and power has been present in human history since Eve's encounter with the serpent in the garden. However, the enshrinement of equality as the basis for a humanistic society is a relatively modern phenomenon and is enjoying its fifteen minutes of fame on the world stage. It is but a bit player in man's long history of ordering his relationships on this planet.

The modern concept of equality is a child of humanism and the humanistic spirit of the world. Always present in the fallen nature of man, the humanistic concept of equality began its ascendance in Christendom during the early Renaissance. The early European Renaissance began with medieval Europe's Crusades in the twelfth and thirteenth centuries which brought it into contact with civilizations much more advanced in learning from classical Greece and Rome. The cataclysmic events of the fourteenth century would further hasten the demise of the medieval Age of Faith. Almost all countries were decimated by war and the Black Plague. One papal inquiry estimated that Europe lost forty million or about a quarter of its population in just five years.[18] Disease and famine fed the European pyre with such magnitude and intensity that it fractured the foundations of society. Political structures changed as new despotisms arose, public and private morality declined precipitously, and commercial interests realigned themselves. By the beginning of the fifteenth century, the later Renaissance brought sweeping intellectual and social changes that finally brought to an end the thousand years of medieval order. The new regime was humanism and continues to our day.[19] And it was the later Renaissance continuing into the sixteenth century that would usher in a new era and challenge man's fundamental way of thinking in the seventeenth and eighteenth centuries.[20]

At the threshold of the new era stood the god of science. And science would divide its attentions between two main arenas: the science of nature and the science of human nature. And it is to the second to which we turn our attention. Thomas Hobbes outlined the main points of the science of human nature in his *Leviathan* in 1651 whose basic principle was sensationalism which rested on the premise that all knowledge and all mental life starts from the reception of sensations external to man. John Locke (1632-1704) was the one who popularized and developed Hobbes' sensationalism.[21] Locke believed that society was the result of a voluntary contract among men equal in a state of nature. Locke's principle work was *Essay on Human Understanding* and its essence was summarized by Russell Kirk.

> ...that the whole of our knowledge is derived from the experience of the individual's five senses. We see, hear, touch, taste, smell: these are our sole sources of information, of knowledge, of wisdom...Moral beliefs are not implanted in human individuals...by any agency superior to the flesh; no, they are learnt through experience of pleasure and pain...[22]

John Herman Randall called this reliance on experience "The omnipotence of Environment."

> ...Since all that men are comes from experience, all present differences and inequalities must be due to differences in environment, and men must *at birth* be exactly equal. Such was the corollary that men drew from sensationalism, the necessary foundation for the democratic faith that men are born equal and that education alone is needed to perfect human life and to bring into being the ideal democratic society. No wonder that the men of the eighteenth century were intensely hopeful of the future: all that is bad is due to a faulty education and a faulty social environment. Once change these, and there is no limit to the possibilities of human nature.[23] [emphasis in original]

From the foundation of Hobbes' sensationalism and its development by Locke, the French were the first to develop democratic ideas of human equality.[24] The ideas of human equality flourished during the period known as the Enlightenment, that period stretching from the late seventeenth century until the end of the eighteenth century. Enlightenment thought centered in France and "... meant the strong intellectual tendency toward doctrines of progress, rationality, secularism, and political reform."[25]

Following a hundred years of enlightenment thought, the French ideas of human equality reached its zenith in the French Revolution. The principles of the Revolution rested on faith in reason which it supposed would "...spread over the entire earth and *result in real economic, social, and intellectual equality*."[26] [emphasis added] This diaspora of reason would allow the unimpeded laws of nature to banish ignorance, intolerance, and parochialism and allow society to be reformed. Resistance to human progress would only come from those wedded to the past or who clung to indefensible privilege. The leaders of the Enlightenment would be the priesthood of the new order because of their "specialized competence" and wear the title of critic, reformer, and intellectual.[27]

Against the perversions of Enlightenment thought stood the biblical worldview. The biblical view of equality predates the French pretentions by seventeen centuries. The Apostle Paul's encounter with the proud Athenians at Mars Hill is one of the most remarkable and unique windows into the history of the clash between the worldviews of humanism and Christianity that continues to dominate in culture wars of the twenty-first century.

Calling him a babbler and a preacher of foreign divinities, the Epicurean and Stoic philosophers laid hold of Paul and brought him to Areopagus to question him more about Jesus and the resurrection which he preached. Paul spoke to the heathens at Mars Hill who worshipped the Unknown God. It was the Unknown God that Paul proclaimed as the Creator and master of human destiny which was sustained and guided through divine power. Paul presented the Creator to the Athenians as

> ...the God that made the world and all things therein...therefore Lord of heaven and earth...*He made of one blood all nations of men*...He giveth to all life, and breath, and all things...He is the sovereign disposer of all the affairs of the children of men...He is not far from every one of us...In him we live, and move, and have our being...and are God's offspring. [Excerpts from John 17:2-28. KJV] [emphasis added]

It was in this discourse that Paul revealed to the Athenians the origin of man as God's offspring and that all nations of men were of one blood. Paul's observation is a foundational concept for the biblical view of equality. However, from a biblical perspective we cannot approach the concept of equality in the same way as does one who adheres to the humanistic worldview of equality (economic, social, and intellectual equality). These concepts are societal constructs of equality which are affixed to man, but they do not reflect the nature of man who was created in the image of God. Rather, man's position in relation to God, society, and each other rests upon the concept of *fraternity*—all nations of men were of one blood. It is in this context that equality is but a poor cousin in the affairs of men. In the biblical worldview, equality has only two voices: equality of man before God and equality of man before God's law.

To establish the truth with regard to equality under the opposing worldviews of Christianity and humanism, one needs a framework to systematically examine in greater detail the tenets of those worldviews. The answers of each worldview as to the basic questions of life can provide this framework and generally fall into a few basic categories.

Every worldview or belief system must answer certain questions: What is the nature and structure of our world and how does it function? Where are we heading? What shall we do (values)? "How should we attain our goals? "What is true and false?"[28]

Charles Colson and Nancy Pearcey, in their book *How Now Shall We Live?* reduces to three questions what any worldview must answer: "Where did we come from, and who are we? What has gone wrong with the world? What can we do to fix it?" Answers to these questions allow one to evaluate any area of life (e.g., religion, family life, politics, science, education, the arts, and popular culture) and determine how these evaluations area aligns with one's worldview.[29] From these answers we can determine which worldview presents the truth about equality in man's quest for the good society.

Equality is essentially a perception about the relationship between two or more separate entities. Therefore, the entire book will be consumed with comparing and contrasting the worldviews of humanism and Christianity with regard to their separate views of equality and its impact on human relationships. Our purpose is to search for the truth about equality by examining the divergent views presented by Christianity and humanism. By doing so we can decide which worldview is most coherent, consistent, and gives orientation and direction for living life, that is, which one reflects reality.

Our goal is to find the worldview that reflects the truth about equality which will lead to the good society. In chapter 1 it was said that the good society is marked by a high degree of *order, justice, and freedom*. But order, justice and freedom cannot be addressed in a mechanistic or detached manner for each is intricately linked and dependent on a right interpretation and operation of the other two as they interact with human nature. In the next three chapters we shall address order, justice, and freedom but also their connection and interaction with each other.

3

Order and the Good Society

A man may exist for a season upon a storm-tossed ocean of societal disorder, but his mind must have order regardless of external circumstances, that is, man must have a coherent orientation to the past, present, and future. To have order he must know truth (reality), and it is the nature of humans to search for truth, to attempt to know what is real. This is well stated by Albert M. Wolters:

> One of the unique characteristics of human beings is that we cannot do without the kind of orientation and guidance that a worldview gives. We need guidance because we are inescapably creatures with responsibility who by nature are incapable of holding purely arbitrary opinions or making entirely unprincipled decisions. We need some creed to live by, some map by which to chart our course. The need for a guiding perspective is basic to human life, perhaps more basic than food or sex.[30]

What is this orientation or creed which we seek that is superior and worthy of being sought to the exclusion of everything else? We call those things eternal truths or norms (also called permanent things or human universals) to which mankind must adhere in order to live. It is a moral order that transcends time. It is not instinct. It is not learned behavior through time although the recognition and practice of those norms are important to keep those norms visible and alive for following generations. Richard Weaver wrote that in both modern cultures and primitive, man has "…powerful feelings of 'oughtness' directed toward the world…"[31]

These feelings of oughtness are compelled by eternal truths or norms that are applicable to all of mankind and to all ages. In God's revelation of the order of the universe to the Hebrews, He pointed back to the beginning of mankind when all men knew of good and evil (See: Genesis 3:22). But as time advanced in the pre-revelation era, man's understanding of good and evil diminished.[32] The revelation to the Hebrews and the first century Christians, recorded over a 1,600-year span of time, gave illumination, order, and meaning to those pre-revelation norms or permanent things that mankind perceived and endeavored to know. Together, the norms or permanent things and the revelation of the order of the universe as created by God are an indispensable component of all human knowing.

In addition to order of the soul (moral order), there must be civic order within society (social order). Once again, we must repeat that moral order and civic order are complementary, intricately linked, and interdependent. Disorder of one leads to disorder of the other.[33] We have briefly touched on the order of the soul and now turn our attention to the collective order of a society (culture) as superbly described by Richard Weaver in chapter 1.

To understand the need for order within a culture and the impact of modern conceptions of equality upon that order, one must understand culture and how it is formed and operates. Culture is a product of the collective consciousness of a group seeing certain felt needs, "...*a complex of values polarized by an image or idea.*" The very foundation of the cultural concept is unity that presupposes a general commonality of thought and action. As a culture (society) is formed and begins ordering its world to bring the satisfactions for which it was created, directions must be imposed on its members. These directions, limits, and required behaviors radiate from a center of authority which exerts a subtle and pervasive pressure to conform. This pressure may range from cultural peer pressure to moral and legal restraints, and those that do not conform are repelled of necessity. Thus, in any culture there are patterns of inclusion and exclusion. Without such patterns, the culture is unprotected and disintegrates over time. Every culture has a central authority which commands all things, and cultures fail and disintegrate without the power to reject that which does not adhere to its central force. Weaver calls this center imaginative rather than logical and "...a focus of value, a law of relationships, an inspiring vision...to which the group is oriented." The intrinsic nature of culture compels that it be exclusive rather than all inclusive. When a culture's complex of values is polarized by an image or idea, we describe this image or idea as its *central cultural vision*, that is, its collective worldview.[34]

Just as an individual's worldview must be based on truth, a culture's central vision must also reflect reality. Thus, we see two unalterable requirements for a culture to survive over time: the culture must have *unity* and must be based on *truth* (reality). Western civilization is experiencing a loss of order (and the basis for unity) as it abandons the Christian worldview which is based on the permanent things (eternal truths, norms, and human universals to which mankind must adhere) and the biblical revelation to the ancient Hebrews and first century Christians.

We have laid the foundation for understanding order and the need for order of the soul and society. In his quest for order, man must know the truth with regard to equality. For Humanists, equality is the natural enemy of hierarchy in human relationships. This can be seen in the diverging views regarding human relationships between the humanist and biblical worldviews. This divergence can be visualized in positional terms: vertical vs. horizontal. As we examine the various descriptions of humanism through its definition, philosophy, application, and worldview, one can see the emphasis on the horizontal (egalitarian) which sharply contrasts with the vertical (biblical hierarchy) with regard to patterns of relationship in all spheres of family and society.

Those holding the Christian worldview believe that both concepts of hierarchy and equality must be applied to human relationships in a manner that reflects the nature of God. For Christians, the primary nature of those relationships is vertical (hierarchical)—God's being is shown by the Father-Son relationship and the relationship of Christ with the Church of which He is the head and His followers are the body. Because man was created in God's image, the hierarchical pattern of relationships is evident in various human institutions and entities throughout history—marriage, family, community, nations, and the Kingdom of God.

Hierarchy implies authority, superior and subordinate, order, and rank. Furthermore, if society is to be understood, it must have structure, and structure requires hierarchy which implies distinctions. Weaver called the "steady obliteration of those distinctions" the most significant omen of our time. Modern society embraces the humanistic perversion that "…in a just society there are no distinctions", but this leads to a loss of cultural identity and ultimately disintegration.[35] In contrast to the humanistic worldview, Weaver described the hierarchical nature of family and its bond with fraternity.

> The ancient feeling of brotherhood carries obligations of which equality knows nothing. It calls for respect and protection, for brotherhood is *status* in family, and family is by nature *hierarchical*…It places people in a network of sentiment, not of rights…[36] [emphasis added]

Equality, rightly applied, is equality before God and the law. But under the humanistic worldview, equality has become a rapacious egalitarianism that imposes regimentation and leveling of circumstance which results in unnatural social groupings. One senses the relentless gravity of the humanistic worldview pulling society downward from hierarchy into a flat (horizontal) social plain and consequent mediocrity. Such humanistic regimentation and leveling of condition result in loss of a sense of belonging and place which leads to suspicion and resentment. From this we see the humanistic definition of equality is a disorganizing concept if we believe that human relationships are the means to achieve order in the soul and society.

If one reflects on the various descriptions of humanism through its definition, philosophy, application, and worldview as given thus far in this book, one can see the emphasis on the horizontal (egalitarian) and the sharp contrasts with the vertical (hierarchical) with regard to relationships in all spheres of family and society. By egalitarian is meant a belief in human equality with special emphasis on *social, political, and economic rights and privileges* and a focus on the removal of any inequalities among humankind.[37] Although humanists champion the freedom of the individual through an equalitarian society, the heart of this philosophy is found in control, regimentation, and conformity. The humanistic concepts of order require socialism as the political and economic means to organize society whose mantra is the "greater good of society" with a consequent regimentation and conformity of individuals within that culture.

Although the humanists' clarion call is for individual freedom, it is evident that in a society ordered around the humanist philosophy the individual must be subordinate to the good of all humanity. But, it is the leaders of the state that determine the definition of what is meant by the "greater good." Ultimately the leaders of a socialistic society rule as they see fit and do so without regard to the individual. Inhabitants of the socialistic system are appeased with promises of equality in their social, political, and economic rights and privileges. However, the price for the humanist' concept of equality is a loss of freedom.

As opposed to a Divine hierarchical social order, humanism's order and organization centers on control and regimentation through a man-created social order which results in oppression. An examination of just a few of humanism's principles will assist in understanding its radical *egalitarian opposition to biblical hierarchy*. Chief among these principles is humanism's insistence on denial of God, a severance that encompasses both time and authority. In other words, God does not now exist nor existed before the appearance of the universe. Creation was a random process of nature; therefore, we are not subject to the authority of some creator. A second example of the leveling aspects of egalitarianism (and denial of hierarchy, rank, and order) in the humanistic worldview regards the *nature of man*. There are no giants upon whose shoulders we stand. Quite the contrary, contemporary man is the latest and greatest model that evolved from the slime pits of the past. As a product of evolution, humankind cannot be fallen nor have need of redemption. If man is not fallen, then there cannot be right and wrong, only different points of view. Man is his own master and owes nothing to a mythical God or the ancients. There is no heaven above nor hell below and therefore no hierarchy, only an everlasting march to an unattainable and unknowable horizon that continually recedes into the distance.[38] Each of these principles preached by humanists fundamentally undermines the ordered existence that has guided mankind since his presence on the planet.

The philosophy of humanism champions an exaltation of self over family, denial of patrimony, emphasis on the present and the experiential, flexible and interchangeable values, life lived for the moment for there is nothing beyond, and deference to the senses. This philosophy represents a *detachment* from any hierarchical bonds of duty, obligation, patrimony, and the permanent things.[39] As shown throughout this book, such detachment leads to disorder of the soul and society.

We have determined that order is one of the fundamental components necessary for an enduring culture. Also, we have determined that order must be built on the foundation of a unified central cultural vision and objective truth. With that understanding of order, we have compared and contrasted the Christian and humanistic worldviews with regard to equality and its impact on order of the soul and society. Our findings are that the humanistic definition of equality undermines the cultural concept of order. Order of the soul is not achieved through the false liberation of the individual from family, duty, obligations, patrimony, and God. Rather, one becomes a prisoner of self, loneliness, mediocrity and despair. The humanistic concept of equality is also a disorganizing and destructive concept in so far as human relationships mean order because it debases the supremacy of the central cultural vision and rejects objective truth which leads to disintegration of society.

4

Justice and the Good Society

As previously stated, Russell Kirk believed justice is one of the "...three fundamental virtues that form the bonds that unite American society, the other two being order and freedom." Order is the first need of society. As a society recognizes certain principles of a tolerable civil order, those principles of order become laws that make justice possible. Justice and the enforcement of laws quell violence and make freedom possible. A just society requires a standard of judgment by which fairness, impartiality, and right action is measured, and this standard of judgment must be above the temper of the moment. This standard of judgment is the law which follows established principles and is no respecter of rank or station. Therefore, we see justice as the critical link between indispensable order and the elixir of freedom. [40]

The ideals of fairness, impartiality, and right action are the stuff of justice, "...the principle or process by which every man and woman in society are accorded the things that are rightfully their own: their lives, their dignity, their property, their station in life." Here we must distinguish between justice and the law. Justice is of a higher order and by its nature involves morality. Justice prevails when the courts of law mirror justice's ethical standards.[41]

Christian worldview of justice

Justice is part of the very character, nature, and being of God. The Bible reveals that He is a just God (See: Deuteronomy 32:4, Isaiah 45:21). Therefore, it follows that the laws flowing from His creative order should reflect His nature and, if so, His laws should be just. Before the revelation man struggled through life searching for principles upon which to order his existence yet fearing a perilous future guided by chance, accident, or the seemingly whimsical and malevolent moods of uncaring gods. But pre-revelation man was not excused from God's justice.

> ...because what may be known of God is manifest in them, for God has shown *it* to them. For since the creation of the world His invisible *attributes* are clearly seen, being understood by the things that are made, *even* His eternal power and Godhead, so that they are without excuse... [Romans 1:19-20. NKJV]

In other words, God was just when He found them guilty of violation of His laws as revealed in nature. It was God's revelation to the ancient Hebrews that brought clarity, definition, and focus to those eternal truths by which man must live. And because God was just and man was created in His image, man had hope for justice on this earth.

The American standard for justice was found in the common law which according to Webster's Dictionary of 1828, was the "rules, principles, and customs which have been received from our ancestors and by which courts have been governed in their judicial decisions."[42] For America, those established principles flowed from a thousand years of Anglo-Saxon common law that arose over centuries of judicial decisions and was derived from the "...experience of people living in community and settling their differences by legal means over a very long period of time." Much of common law flowed from natural law, a set of norms that derive from an authority above the state and "...pertains to a people's culture across the whole of life, not to matters of law merely." Statutory law developed later to address situations in which common law was viewed as inadequate.[43] It is through the convolutions and inventions of statutory law by humanistic liberals and progressives that great damage has been done to the restraining standards of the common law heritage of the United States.

Supreme Court Justice Joseph Story, appointed by President Madison, unequivocally connected the centrality of Christianity and the common law in the founding of America. "I verily believe Christianity necessary to the support of civil society. One of the beautiful boasts of our municipal jurisprudence is that Christianity is a part of the Common Law... There never has been a period in which the Common Law did not recognize Christianity as lying its foundations...I verily believe Christianity necessary to the support of civil society."[44] And it was from the authority of the common law resting on God's laws that justice was dispensed.

Humanist worldview of justice

Justice for the humanist derives *not* from the long centuries of human interaction that created standards of fairness, impartiality, and right action. Rather, humanists construct a definition of justice to fit their worldview in which man is merely an economic being. Jim Herrick quotes John Rawls who wrote in *A Theory of Justice* that, "All social values – liberty and opportunity, income and wealth, and the bases of self-respect – are to be distributed equally unless an unequal distribution of any, or all of these values is to everyone's advantage." Herrick continues, "The legitimacy for such a society is not a god, or the rule of a king, or even the rule of a powerful clique. It is as if *we construct* society according to an imaginary contract that *all rational citizens* could have made. *Justice means that there is a fair measure of economic distribution.*"[45] [emphasis added]

Numerous objections and questions arise with regard to Rawls' and Herrick's admonitions. Why is it fair to take one man's property and give it to another? By whose authority does Rawls dictate an equal distribution of income and wealth? He says such authority flows not from a god or king. For Herrick, that authority lies with all rational citizens that would grant mental assent to such a society constructed from the imagination. Thus, when Herrick says "we construct", he means those rational citizens who are the conditioners of society—those who decide what and how income and wealth will be distributed.

This is at the heart of humanism's flawed concept of justice whose standard is man's determination of a "fair measure of economic distribution." Who decides what is fair, impartial, and right in the pursuit of justice? Under humanist definitions, justice is of human construction and subject to the tenor of the times, the current interpretations of evolving truth, and the judgments of the current cultural elites vested with the power to decide. In such a world justice is a moving target in a sea of relativism and subject to the rudderless whims of corruptible man.

Ignoring the lessons of history, the levelers of society admonish Dame Justice to peak beneath her blindfold and act arbitrarily and capriciously to impose the latest standards dictated by the passions of the moment. Prescriptions of fairness, impartiality, and right action derived from an authority above the state and built up over the centuries are now considered quaint, failing to keep up with modern times, or just plain wrong-headed. In other words, the definition of justice has been changed by the humanists to fit their worldview. But, like order and freedom, justice is not of human construction, and no amount of humanist tinkering will change the heart of man with regard to a right understanding of fairness, impartiality, and right action in a civil society. Societies that ignore the true meaning of justice do so at their peril as respect for law and its rule are diminished.

The concept of justice is a universal truth, a thing of permanence or status that transcends the whole of man's time on this planet and pertains to all cultures. When a culture "…by ignorant popular attitudes or by social derangements" imposes a political concept that creates a different principle of ordering society contrary to universal truths, dissatisfactions arise because society has tampered with the 'nature of things.'"[46] No longer having permanence (status), justice has moved to the realm of function (a tool for change). It is in this realm that justice becomes a political concept devoid of fixed reference points and thus allows the ordering of society to be made consistent with the humanist worldview.

Justice breeds respect…respect for authority, property rights, institutions, customs, and traditions, and to regard with esteem people who share that understanding of justice. But, *equality that pretends to insure justice is inherently unjust in doing so.* And *forced* equality's injustice is inevitably corrosive to human relationships and leads to loss of respect and unity in all facets of society.

As we have seen, order allows the establishment of laws that support order. From just laws, justice is made possible, and from the possibility of justice flow freedom. But when the indispensable *link* of justice is detached from status or permanence in the zealous pursuit of humanistic definitions of equality, a culture's order and freedom disintegrate over time. In reality, humanistic equalitarianism is a thief of status, property, patrimony, and ultimately freedom. In such is not found justice.

5

Freedom and the Good Society

Richard Weaver has applied the terms *status* and *function* in describing the general aspects of a culture. By "status" he means the feature of permanence anchored in timeless values and basic laws. By "function" he means that of change. A culture achieves rewarding social structures and works of imagination only where there can be found equilibrium between status and function. To put it another way, there is a dynamic tension between permanence and change. Things change over time, but these are nuanced changes that merely refine and do not change the substance, the idea, or the nature of a thing. However, Weaver observed that in the modern world there has been a loss of equilibrium as function has displaced status.[47] We have become a nation of compulsive social engineers attempting to fix society's ills rather than look for answers in those timeless values associated with status. The mechanic's tools in modernism's predisposition for function are political concepts unhooked from timeless values and laws. These man-invented political concepts impose demands in the form of laws and regulations administered by an omnipresent and ceaseless bureaucracy in areas where other means of ordering are proper. A culture's neglect of status in favor of function results in a *loss of freedom*.

Humanism's definition of equality is perhaps the foremost of those political concepts that tramples status in favor of function and therefore is detached from timeless values and laws. In the modern world, equality has become politicized, redefined, and deified (the humanist will wince at the use of a word implying the supernatural) and as a result has caused great damage to society. Much like democracy, the concept of equality has been infused with ethereal qualities of innate goodness and utility that supposedly operates, if allowed, with magical curative powers within an ailing society. Yet, a society consumed with equality is continually in a state of flux, and the pursuit of progress and perfectibility bring about the very inequities that a humanistic society detests. Thus, function (change) becomes the master as status (permanence) is discarded. The resulting loss of equilibrium places a culture on the road to disintegration.

Humanism's new definition of equality created disequilibrium between equality and those timeless values and basic laws of human nature. It also disrupts equality's equilibrium with concepts such as freedom long understood and valued by man.

To understand the Christian worldview as it relates to freedom, we must examine God's creation of man. As previously stated, man was created with God's divine image stamped upon him. Man has an insatiable thirst for freedom because God made man with freewill. Simply put, freedom means an absence of coercion and constraint. Also, the freedom granted man did not mean an absence of consequences for disobeying God. The consequences of disobedience to God's laws are readily evident in society, but those consequences should not be confused with coercion or lack of freedom. Man must suffer the consequences for wrong choices. As he joins himself with his like-minded fellowmen in an organized society, they voluntarily impose restrictions on themselves to make life better. It is a freedom to restrain one's self.

If, as we have said, a culture neglects status in favor of function, there is a loss of freedom. This truth creates a huge public relations problem for humanists in selling their philosophy. Humanism's equality conflicts with man's understanding of freedom in two ways. First, the humanistic concept of freedom must allow for a measure of coercion so that equality may be imposed, but this coercion conflicts with man's innate understanding that freedom means an absence of coercion. Second, humanism promises to free man from the constraints of mores, norms, traditions, distant voices of the past, and ultimately God. However, humanists must overcome man's innate understanding of the painful consequences that result when behavior violates those timeless principles. What is the poor humanist to do?

Humanism's answer to its first problem of man's true understanding of freedom is to dethrone freedom from its ancient *status* and replace it with *function*. Freedom now functions in culture as an agent of change to create a society whose central cultural vision reflects the humanist philosophy. This bait and switch tactic allows the imposition of equality into areas where it is not meant to be. To make one's new restrained freedom amenable to imposed equality, man is appeased with economic, social rights and privileges which the narcissistic populace gladly exchanges for the old freedom concerned only with absence of coercion.

The humanists' second problem is man's understanding of the consequences of violating unchangeable concepts of right and wrong. Again, the humanists' answers by redefining objective truth to be relativistic so that man may be liberated from the strictures of morality, mores, norms, and religion by giving unbridled expression to his self and senses. The painful consequences of liberating man's sensual nature are blamed on continued pockets of inequality and intolerance which mandate even more social engineering by the cultural elites. To counter the death spiral into cultural disorder caused by a false understanding of freedom, the statists impose an ever greater array of laws, regulations, rules, policies, procedures, guidelines, and directives in attempts to stamp out ever increasing levels of unrest caused by *perceived* inequalities and intolerance. But, this inevitably leads to an ever-increasing loss of freedom for the inmates of that society.

Men trade their true freedom for humanism's lawlessness falsely labeled as freedom. Freedom has become "freedom to" (doing) as opposed to the ancient concept of "freedom from" coercion (being). But man has failed to read the fine print in his bargain with humanism. Humanism's promise of freedom requires individual autonomy to be *consonant with social responsibility* by which is meant that individual freedoms are subordinate to the good of all humanity. Put another way, humanists harness an individual's dignity, worth, and freedom to the principle of the greatest-happiness-for-the greatest-number which is then hitched to the humanist belief that the highest moral obligation is to humanity as a whole. In other words, freedom of the individual is subservient to his obligations to the larger society, and those obligations are determined and defined by the humanist intellectual elite as they see fit without regard to the individual. In the humanists' world, man replaces God as the defining authority for truth. Thereafter, man's highest moral obligation is to humanity as a whole and not to God.

About 190 years ago a young Frenchman prophetically diagnosed the disease that would ultimately lead to America's current cultural disintegration through egalitarianism—regimentation, leveling of society, and unnatural social groupings. Alexis de Tocqueville's *Democracy in America* has been called by some the best book ever written on American democracy. Tocqueville talked of how a nation such as America could come under the establishment of a particular despotism with unusual ease and examined by what means and under what circumstances this new despotism might appear in the world. Tocqueville described how the despotism would use the *seductive allure of equality* as the means to anesthetize man's innate thirst for freedom and enslave him.

> I see an innumerable crowd of men, *all alike and equal*, turned in upon themselves in a restless search for those petty, vulgar pleasures with which they fill their souls. Each of them living apart, is almost unaware of the destiny of all the rest. His children and personal friends are for him the whole of the human race; as for the remainder of his fellow citizens, he stands alongside them but does not see them; he touches them without feeling them; he exists only in himself and for himself; if he still retains his family circle, at any rate he is said to have lost his country.
>
> Above these men stands an immense and protective power which alone is responsible for looking after their

enjoyments and watching over their destiny. It is absolute, meticulous, ordered, provident, and kindly disposed. It would be like a fatherly authority, if, father-like, its aim were to prepare men for manhood, but it seeks only to keep them in perpetual childhood; it prefers its citizens to enjoy themselves provided they have only enjoyment in mind. It works readily for their happiness but it wishes to be the only provider and judge of it. It provides their security, anticipates and guarantees their needs, supplies their pleasures, directs their principal concerns, manages their estates, divides their inheritances. Why can it not remove from them entirely the bother of thinking and the troubles of life?

Thus, it reduces daily the value and frequency of the exercise of free choice; it restricts the activity of free will within a narrower range and gradually removes autonomy itself from each citizen. *Equality has prepared men for all this, inclining them to tolerate all these things and often see them as a blessing.*[48] [emphasis added]

Man alone among all creatures was created with a free will and his human nature thirsts for freedom. Once again we see the deleterious effects of humanism's equality which erodes human freedom and attempts to quench his innate thirst for such freedom through "….petty, vulgar pleasures with which they fill their souls." As a society embraces humanism's equality, its citizens are imprisoned in socialism's velvet gulag. Lord Acton captured the essence of the loss of freedom to equality when he said, "The finest opportunity ever given to the world was thrown away because the *passion for equality* made vain the hope for freedom."[49] [emphasis added]

Part II – Equality and Human Relationships

Part I may be deemed somewhat general in nature and perhaps a bit theoretical and/or academic, but it was necessary to describe the structural components of a good society (order, justice, freedom) as a foundation for understanding the disordering and disintegrative impact of embracing modern humanistic concepts of equality in each sphere of life.

In Part II we will demonstrate the degradation of the good society as a consequence of *applied* humanism as it relates to everyday life of America in the grip of *forced* equality. Humanistic concepts of equality are presented as superior but are not when examined in light of its destruction of society and the consequent loss of order, justice, and freedom.

Egalitarianism's *forced* equality is achieved by trashing the eternal truths, universals, norms, and mores and traditions of the Judeo-Christian worldview. The once prevailing good society is reduced to chaos, poverty, injustice, and bondage. With eyes blinded and minds deceived, they shout "your way is no better than mine!" First comes anarchy, then the masses are ready to accept an imposed order without justice or freedom. An impoverished totalitarian order devoid of justice and freedom is achieved except for the privileged overseers who manage the gulags.

6

Equality and the God-Man Relationship

Since this book deals with the concept of equality in Western civilization, we will confine our comments to the rival conceptions of truth as presented by the prevailing dominant worldviews—Christianity and humanism. As discussed earlier, the perspective from which one views equality cannot be fully understood apart from an examination of his or her worldview. Put another way, one's worldview determines how he or she reacts to other aspects of society, that is, human relationships. Worldview is one's conception of how the world works, that is, one's conception of what is truth or reality. A faulty worldview results in a distorted or warped perspective. Therefore, as we examine the rival concepts of equality's role in human life, we must test the competing claims of Christianity and Humanism to determine which of those claims support truth or reality.

A fundamental demarcation that separates worldviews begins with belief as to the existence or non-existence of a supreme being or, as C. S. Lewis described in his book *Mere Christianity*, the "The Rival Conceptions of God." The first major division of mankind is between those who believe in some kind of God or gods and those who do not. Lewis rightly states that the majority believe in a god of some form or fashion. Lewis further divides the believers based on the nature of the God in which they believe. As to this nature, there are those that believe that God is beyond good and evil (pantheism) and those that believe God is good or righteous. Pantheists believe God animates the universe and is almost the totality of the universe. If the universe ceased to exist, so would the Pantheists' God. Therefore, everything found in the universe is part of God. As opposed to pantheistic belief that God is beyond good and evil, Christians, Jews, and Mohammedans hold the view that God is good.[50]

A society's perspective from which it views equality is a product of the collective worldviews of its inhabitants, that is, its central cultural vision. This is important because the Christian-humanist disagreement as to the existence of God results in vast differences in understanding the concept of equality and its role in Western civilization. For those that believe in the God of the Bible, there is only one source that can give the sharpness and clarity of vision that reveals the truth of equality's role in man's life and relationships. For those that hold a humanistic worldview, God does not exist and equality's role in human existence is determined by man himself unshackled from unchanging eternal truths and distant voices of the past. Society's choice between those two rival perspectives from which equality is viewed and defined leads to dramatically different outcomes regarding the type of society in which its citizens will live and die.

Equality by its very nature means more than one and implies relationship. Therefore, a discussion of equality among humans and its role in society is meaningless without an understanding of *relationships*—the Christian conception of man's relationship with the supernatural God and the humanist rejection of that God. Whether one believes that God exists or not dramatically impacts his or her relationship with other humans.

For those that believe in God, all of mankind's relational patterns are designed, established, and modeled by God. However, God has given man freewill, and he may choose to violate those pre-ordained relational patterns. Humanists deny such a God and therefore their personal interactions and relational patterns with other human and community relationships are more ephemeral and non-specific. Humanistic relationships are defined and driven by man-made philosophical considerations as opposed to the unchanging nature of man throughout his history on the earth. Ultimately, humanists view themselves as citizens of the world community unshackled from nationalistic loyalties, concerns, and boundaries.

The Christian view of the God-man relationship

As we shall see, God is big on imagery. Why? Because He wants us to know Him. He tells us that we were created in His image: "Then God said, "Let Us make man in Our image, according to Our likeness..." [Genesis 1:26a. NKJV] Notice the implicit Trinitarian imagery. This imagery extends beyond the Godhead. We see this triadic pattern impressed upon the various facets of His creation: man (mind, body, soul), the church (Christ, leaders, and the congregants), the family (father, mother, and children), the state (God, ruler/administrator, citizens), laws governing behavior (physical, spiritual, and social), the economy (God, man, material things), the sphere of labor (owner, worker, material things), and community (Christ, neighbors, and the needy).[51] In each of these arenas of life, there can be harmony and equilibrium or there can be discord and instability. The outcome depends on h*ow well the actions of men mirror the Creator's image* stamped on those spheres of life. In other words, man has the option to create harmony or discord between the elements of each triadic pattern in society.

Considering the various triatic relationships, we must begin with the Christian conception of man's relationship with God and equality's proper place and role in that relationship. The account of the God-man relationship is spread throughout the Bible. In chapter 3, we briefly mentioned the fundamental need of mankind for relationships, that is, a need to dwell together with other humans. For the Christian, the importance of human relationships is a reflection and derivative of the Trinitarian relationship.

An understanding of these earthly relational patterns of man can be seen through an examination of the nature of God as revealed in the Bible. The concept of the Trinity is immensely important if we are to understand Christianity and how we (mankind) fit into the grand scheme of things (including an understanding of the principal subject of this book: humanism's faulty concept of equality and its impact on society). Christianity is unique in all of the world's religions in that it is Trinitarian. This is profoundly important for without the Trinitarian God, Christianity is an unworkable religion that cannot support its claim as the only religion to present reality (truth). Some object to the use of word "religion" when describing Christianity, but the epitome of all religions is man's search for God. And in the Christian religion, our search has led us to truth which is the God of the Bible.

In John's first epistle, he states, "He who does not love does not know God, for God is love." [1 John 4:8. NKJV] That is Christianity's claim, and no other religion can legitimately make that claim. If God is not Trinitarian, then He must be unipersonal. However, love could not exist until the unipersonal God created another being. Love can only exist between two beings, that is, there must be the possibility of relationship for love to be expressed. If a unipersonal God made man in his image (as did the God of the Bible), that image cannot contain relational patterns because of that God's unipersonality. Therefore, man would not have need for relationship. Some may argue that even if God were unipersonal, he was God and had the power to create man with a need for relationship. If that were possible, man would be something *different* from the God he serves, and this unipersonal God would be *alien* to man's understanding of his own nature which craves relationship. If the unipersonal God is alien, how is man to know and serve the unipersonal God without knowing the nature and expectations of that God? He cannot, and religion (man's search for God) will be fruitless and frustrating as man stumbles through life in a blind, pointless quest for meaning and purpose. Thus, we see the importance and necessity of the Triune God.

As we begin to have a hint of understanding of the Trinitarian relationship, our finite mental powers are overwhelmed with astonishment at the utter magnitude and reality that God chose to share the divine relationship his special creation—mankind. Another word for reality is truth, and with regard to truth there can be no comparisons of Christianity with other religions and philosophies. We cannot say Christianity is just truer than other religions for there are no degrees of truth and falseness within Christianity or between Christianity and other religions and philosophies. Christianity is perfectly, completely, and eternally true. In other words, Christ is truth.

Early church fathers used the concept of perichoresis, a Greek word, to describe the Trinitarian relationship of God the Father, Jesus the Son, and the Holy Spirit. The meaning of this concept came from the peers of the early church (Basil, Gregory of Nazianzus, Gregory of Nyssa and others). Perichoresis explains the close interrelatedness of the Father, Son, and Holy Spirit, each of which is clearly distinct but at the same time "…one in their own eternal and intense love for each other."[52] Expressed another way, it is one heart beating within three persons.

Hilary of Poitiers was a fourth century Frenchman and an early and staunch defender of correct theology in the church. He described the inner-workings of the Trinity: "Three Beings can reciprocally contain One Another, so that One should permanently envelope, and also be permanently enveloped by the Other, whom yet He envelopes."[53]

Perichoresis shares its etymological roots with the word "choreography."[54] With this in mind, Timothy Keller, in his book *The Reason for God*, wonderfully adds to our understanding of this relationship which he calls the Dance of God. The dance is about love and relationship which implies constant movement or flowing in which a "…self-giving love is the dynamic currency of the Trinitarian life of God. Three persons within God exalt, commune with, and defer to one another…a dynamic pulsating activity, a life, a kind of drama…a kind of dance…"[55]

And God has allowed man to share in this Trinitarian relationship. How can we know this? John's gospel gives us the answer in Christ's own words: "And the glory which You gave Me I have given them, that they may be one just as We are one: I in them, and You in Me; that they may be made perfect in one." [John 17: 22-23a. NKJV] Historian George Marsden summarized Jonathan Edwards's explanation of this passage. "The ultimate reason that God creates, said Edwards, is not to remedy some lack in God, but to extend that perfect internal communication of the triune God's goodness and love…" Keller refines Edward's statement when he said, "God did not create us *to get* the cosmic, infinite joy of mutual love and glorification, but *to share* it.[56] [emphasis added]

By contrast, the humanistic understanding of man rests on the *primacy of self* as opposed to relationship and results in self-centeredness and egotism which is hostile to the divine pattern of relational self-giving. The humanists' solo dance of self is devoid of needed sustenance to feed mankind's universal hunger for love, relationship, purpose, and meaning.

For the Christian, how does the concept of equality enter into the equation as it relates to the God-man relationship? We begin with Paul's letter to the Romans.

> For as many as are led by the Spirit of God, these are sons of God. For you did not receive the spirit of bondage again to fear, but you received the Spirit of adoption by whom we cry out, "Abba, Father." The Spirit Himself bears witness with our spirit that we are children of God, and if children, then heirs—heirs of God and joint heirs with Christ, if indeed we suffer with *Him,* that we may also be glorified together. [Romans 8:14-17. NKJV]

Paul's words do not imply that there has been a change in rank or station between God and man who receives sonship. This restoration of relationship is not a narrowing of the gap between the Creator's deity and His special creation in order to reflect a higher degree of equality. Rather, man is led by the Spirit and may through freewill freely choose to accept the spirit of sonship and be *adopted* into the family of God. As Matthew Henry wrote, "A sanctified (purified) soul bears the image of God, as the child bears the image of the father."[57] Man has achieved status in the family of God, but sonship does not change but enhances the hierarchal nature of relationship with God that once was broken.

Humanism's denial of the God-man relationship

With regard to humanism's concept of equality and its proper role in society, a discussion of a God-man relationship has no meaning or significance for the humanist because of his denial of the existence of a supreme being that created the universe and all therein. But our discussion of the God-man relationship has not been wasted. First, a correct understanding of the triune nature of God and his relationship to man is essential as we explore other human relationships. Second, even though humanists deny the existence of God, in reality they have replaced the supernatural God with one of their own—man himself. Thus, humanistic man worships at the altar of *self.* In this light we shall now examine humanism's God-man relationship, that is, man's homage to himself. It is in the exaltation of self that we shall connect the roots of humanistic belief to modern humanism's conception of equality.

Through the ages there has been a succession of philosophers that attempted to define things and existence apart from God. Although they served many gods, the masters of this quest for truth apart from the supernatural were the Greeks whose pre-eminent civilization existed five centuries before the birth of Christ. In his massive volume *The New History of the World,* J. N. Roberts praised the accomplishments of the ancient Greeks.

> ...there is a salient theme which emerges in it: a growing confidence in rational, conscious enquiry. If civilization is advance towards the control of mentality and environment by reason, then the Greeks did more for it than any of their predecessors. They invented the philosophical question as part and parcel of one of the great intuitions of all time, that a coherent and logical explanation of things could be found, that the world did not ultimately rest upon the meaningless and arbitrary fiat of gods or demons...the liberating effect of this emphasis was felt again and again for thousands of years. It was the greatest single Greek achievement.[58]

From these first questionings came a succession of philosophers that built the foundations of modern humanism. Protagoras (481-411 BC) in his *Of the Gods* claimed that man could not know whether gods existed or not, and in all cases such were not relevant to man. He would famously define man as "... *the measure of all things,* of the reality of those which are, and the unreality of those which are not."[59] [emphasis added]

However, man's arrogant pride and self-confidence that fueled the rational, conscious inquiry for the explanation of things apart from God was evident long before the coming of the fifth century BC Greek philosophers.

> And the woman said to the serpent, "We may eat the fruit of the trees of the garden; but of the fruit of the tree which *is* in the midst of the garden, God has said, 'You shall not eat it, nor shall you touch it, lest you die.' Then the serpent said to the woman, 'You will not surely die. For God knows that in the day you eat of it your eyes will be opened, and you will be like God, knowing good and evil.'" [Genesis 3:2-5 KJV. [emphasis added]

The following is a quote from the author's *Ye shall be as gods...* which identifies the first seeds of humanism's pride of self that infected mankind and the consequences thereof.

> This temptation became the first dark cloud on the horizon of man's idyllic existence in the unfolding drama that ended with his fall and separation from his maker. The serpent's whispered words were the seeds of humanism planted in the fertile field of man's free will. Sensual man was the victor that day for the fruit of humanism was pleasant to the eye and good to eat. The

serpent sealed the deal with an offer of wisdom to tempt the root of pride within man. Sweet revenge the serpent chuckled. The pride that cost him his place in the heavens would now rob God of his precious creation. The serpent had rebelled against God and was cast down. Now man had rebelled and was cast out and separated from God for whom he had been created. Henceforth in sorrow and by the sweat of his brow, man must wrest from the cursed ground the herb of the field amidst thorns and thistles. At the end of his days he discovered another of the serpent's lies that had been mixed with truth—he would surely die.[60]

This self-absorbed humanistic spirit has existed in man since that fateful day in Paradise, but it was the Greeks that gave humanism its form and substance as a philosophical means for man to replace God as the source for explaining and ordering life.

Two fundamental concepts define the entire structural differences between the worldviews of Christianity and humanism—man's origins and man's nature. In the Christian worldview, we have previously identified God as the supreme creator of the universe and man as his special creation. Because of man's rebellion against God, man's nature is fallen and has a broken relationship with God as a consequence of his fall.

In the humanistic worldview, man and other life forms are merely products of a long evolutionary cycle that has occurred over billions of years. Moral standards are merely a social byproduct that evolved through human association. Sin, soul, and conscience are ancient myths arising from superstitions that have been replaced by an understanding that man is directed by instincts and drives that evolved through time. Man's reason is a slave to desires and passions and therefore man does not have free choice or free will. If man does not have free choice, then he cannot be judged for his behavior. And without an unchanging measure by which to judge behavior as right or wrong, then there can be no absolutes and therefore no restraints on passions which rule reason. Man is not fallen and in need of redemption. Rather, man is continuously perfectible and over time will progressively become better and better.

We shall examine humanism's God-man relationship with regard to both *society* and the *individual*. It is at this juncture we must ask how a society's progress and success is defined and achieved in the humanist worldview. The articulation of a *new social order* was made by the Enlightenment philosophers of the eighteenth century. The pinnacle of Enlightenment thought lay in the *Encyclopedie,* the twenty-one volume repository of knowledge and propaganda of the French philosophers whose publication stretched from 1751 to 1765. Guided by the now codified philosophy of humanism, the enlightened thinking of man would make possible this new social order. Ignorance, intolerance, and parochialism were to be exorcised from society as "...the unimpeded operations of the laws of nature, uncovered by reason, would promote the reform of society in everyone's interest except those wedded to the past by their blindness and their enjoyment of indefensible privilege."[61]

In this ideal society, science and reason would lead the way. Progress toward this ideal society would be achieved through education. John Herman Randall, Jr. captured the essence of the idea of progress as championed by the Enlightenment philosophers.

> So long as men continue to accumulate knowledge, progress will be as inevitable as the growth of a tree; nor is there any reason to look for its cessation…The principles of the Revolution, that is, of eighteenth century faith in reason, will spread over the entire earth; liberty and *equality, a real economic and social and intellectual equality*, will be continually strengthened; peace will reign on earth…"[62] [emphasis added]

It is here we see the beginnings of an articulation of the modern humanist's concept of equality. It was the French who developed the democratic ideals of human equality which were based on the assumption of the perfectibility of man. If we follow the logical progression of perfectibility, we must assume men were equal at birth. If equal at birth, what men became was due to environment (their experiences in life). A bad environment (experiences) produced inequalities and differences. Such an environment was the source of injustice, turmoil, crime, poverty, and a host of other social ills. To achieve the ideal democratic society man must be educated to change the environment by eliminating all inequalities and differences.

Out of this Enlightenment thinking came the French Revolutionaries' rallying cry of "liberty, equality, fraternity." The French philosophers' optimistic doctrine of human goodness became the foundation of the French Revolution whereas the American founders' relied on a biblical view of man. The French relied on the insubstantial timber of equality inserted between the planks of liberty and fraternity whereas the Americans relied on order that rested upon "a respect for prescriptive rights and customs." The leveling theories of French radicalism led to anarchy, the Terror, and autocracy while the biblical view of man led to the Constitution of 1787.[63]

The humanist god was man. Enlightenment philosophers attempted to conform redefined man to humanism's new social order but ignored the realities of his true nature present since the beginning of his time on the earth.

We now turn from humanism's God-man relationship with the new social order to man himself. Humanism's ideal democratic society must be populated with the ideal perfectible man. Having told man he is basically good, man must be educated so that he will be a good citizen of the world by conforming to the new social order. His educators will inform him of how he must think, believe, and act. Man's reward for abandonment of freewill is a release of his sensual side supposedly repressed by the customs, values, traditions, morals and principles dictated by non-existent gods, ageless voices from the past, and antique religions.

Having found man has an innate understanding of right and wrong and does not easily reject the wisdom of the ancients in favor of the sensual self, humanists turned to science and reason to convince man that he can and must find happiness in this life for there is no hereafter. Abraham Maslow and other popular apostles of humanism in the 1970s sought to lead the way through humanistic education. Teachers were taught to view each child as an *autonomous self* who "...must create their own purpose by making choices, even though there is no standard to tell them whether or not the choices they are making are right."[64] Never mind that ancient bromide, "Children, obey your parents in the Lord, for this is right." [Ephesians 6:1. NKJV] The autonomous self is thus freed from supposed psychological barriers erected by parents, religion, mores and traditions, and distant voices of the past so that the autonomous self can become an autonomous decision maker.

In 1943, Maslow developed his now famous theory of a "hierarchy of human needs" portrayed as a pyramid which equates an individual's greatest happiness with the fulfillment of needs at the highest possible level. According to Maslow, the higher one ascends on the pyramid, the greater his or her happiness and fulfillment.

> 5. Self-Actualization – Morality, creativity, spontaneity, problem solving, lack of prejudice, and acceptance of facts. Self-actualizers are people who strive for and reach a maximum degree of their inborn potential.
>
> 4. Esteem – Self-esteem, confidence, achievement, respect of others, and respect by others.
>
> 3. Love/Belonging – Friendship, family, sexual intimacy.
>
> 2. Safety – Security of body, employment, resources, morality, the family, health, property.

1. Physiological – Breathing, food, water, sex, sleep, homeostasis, excretion.[65]

In Maslow's hierarchy, the sex act is labeled as a non-relational physiological need and banished to the lowest level of the hierarchy. Family at the second level is merely for safety's sake and non-relational. At this level, morality is mere adherence to an understood level of acceptable group behavior but not fixed or decreed by any higher authority. Maslow's morality at the highest level is somewhat similar to that of level two, but the authority that determines acceptable behavior is now the humanistic state whose moral standards are subject to change at the whim of its leaders and the self-proclaimed elite. The bottom two levels deal with physiological and safety needs and are not so much motivational options to be contemplated but survival and coping mechanisms. What separates man from the animal kingdom are the concepts at the three highest levels of Maslow's pyramid. The two highest deal with self and are inward looking and tend to egotism. It is only at level three of the hierarchy that we see the relational needs of family, friendship, and sexual intimacy which are outward looking.

For individuals in a humanistic society of autonomous selves, the greatest happiness is found as they climb beyond relational needs and achieve self-actualization. To be self-actualized is to be self-fulfilled, to reach one's maximum potential. No one is to judge their choices, but neither are they allowed to judge others. All choices are unhooked from concepts of right and wrong or good and evil. The anthem of the self-actualizers is that old Frank Sinatra standard in which he croons, "I did it my way."

Under Maslow's theory, man achieves maximum happiness when he focuses on his personal desires, wants, and ambitions—the self. However, Maslow's theories of human motivation fail because they dramatically diminish the importance of relationship in favor of self. Effectively, Maslow's hierarchy of needs that promotes self and relationship are ordered incorrectly because it conflicts with the mankind's universal primacy of relationship in motivating human beings as opposed to self-centeredness and egotism.

When ordering society, humanism demands leveling (equality) as prerequisite for achieving its egalitarian ideal. No longer is society's central cultural vision a synthesis of the collective worldviews of its citizens. Rather, the state has erected a new social order ruled by the goddess of equality to which the assemblage of autonomous selves must bow. Because all societies are in a continuous state of change and fluctuation which constantly unbalances the newly leveled social order, society must constantly be re-leveled. Therefore, the humanistic state inundates its citizens with a blizzard of burdensome, restrictive, and petty rules, regulations, laws, codes, policies, and directives as they plod forward in an escalating and never-ending quest for political, social, and economic equality. Because the ideal egalitarian state will never be achieved, the new social order's coveted progress of man is mere erratic movement without purpose or destination.

Much of societal disorder that permeates the entire planet is a result of the widely held humanistic worldview's denial of God and misunderstanding of man's fallen nature. From this faulty worldview, self has been elevated above relationships. And the engine driving this chaotic worldview is the quest for equality that demands a leveling of society which in turn can be achieved only through socialism. Therefore, humanism's imposition of equality as a means of ordering society is fatally flawed in that it is incompatible with the nature of man and his understanding of true liberty. We close this chapter with an excerpt from a book written by the author which describes the consequences to a society that surrenders to a tedious existence under the rule of a small cadre of oppressive humanist overseers—an imposed order without justice and freedom.

> To consider humans as the children of God is abhorrent to social Darwinists. Denying this truth and spurred by belief in the perfectibility of man, scientists seek to know man himself and society. Perhaps it was inevitable that the methods used in the natural and biological sciences would be confidently extended to the affairs of mankind. If the universe is a vast machine run by natural laws, then those laws would operate with regard to man and society. Thus, scientism—the rational application of scientific theories and methods of the natural sciences to society and politics—would allow mankind to sweep away the ills of society including ignorance, poverty, war, hatred, and crime. Scientism took its cue from evolutionary biology and viewed man as an animal that evolved over the ages. Man and society could be studied, understood, manipulated, and improved. Man would no longer be limited by imaginary concepts of right and wrong as he is merely a bundle of instincts and urges. Learned responses were responsible for flaws in human nature, not moral corruption. No longer would the barometer of conscience be allowed to guide and restrain. Without a conscience, could there be a need for moral reasoning and moral responsibility? And of the soul, enlightened man has no need. But then again, the promise of this brave new world comes with a price. We may be a little less human, the malaise of life a little

greater, but we shall have bread, security, imposed structure, and…boredom. However, we can rest assured that the social scientists, technocrats, and bureaucrats will do their very best for us as we are being perfected.[66]

7

Equality and Marriage-Family Relationships

Before we can determine the proper role of equality in marriage and family relationships, we shall briefly describe the fundamental positions of the worldviews of Christianity and humanism with regard to those fundamental relationships. When we speak of marriage and family relationships, we must also speak of the roles of men and women. It is more than a symbiotic relationship; they are inseparable. One cannot be fully understood without an understanding of the other. To injure one is to injure the other.

The Christian's position is that marriage and family *were created by God* and designed to mirror the triune relationship. Because this design was impressed on all of mankind, marriage and the nuclear family relationships are universals and fundamental anchors of all societies in every age and culture.

Humanism denies the existence of God and therefore must deny that marriage and family relationships are universals. Rather, *such relationships are considered to be "social constructions"* and result "…because religious or political forces of a culture demand that it be that way. There is nothing 'natural' about the family. It is established, crafted, and molded according to what a particular society believes and wants."[67]

The Christian view of marriage and family relationships

We begin with the Christian worldview that marriage and family relationships are designed by God and are a human universal. As with the God-man relationship, the Christian worldview of marriage and family relationships is primarily hierarchical. In other words, marriage and family relationships are a reflection of the Father-Son relationship and the relationship of Christ with the Church of which He is the head and His followers are the body.

Very early in the story of creation, God informs us of the importance of the marriage relationship. "And the LORD God said, "*It is not good that man should be alone; I will make him a helper comparable to him.*" [Genesis 2:18a. NKJV] "Not good" did not mean that God made a mistake in His creation, that something was less than perfect. Rather, God's perfect plan was incomplete or unfinished. Something was missing. Man was alone and that was not good. Being alone, man could not reflect the Trinitarian pattern of the Godhead. Thus, God said, "I will make him a helper comparable to him." [Genesis 2:18b. NKJV] We should note that Eve was not one of God's creatures that He took off the shelf and gave to Adam to appease his loneliness. Instead, God specially crafted and fitted her for Adam. Eve became Adam's wife, and together they became one flesh, a union separate and distinct from any other earthy relationships. Thus, God's plan was for a man and woman to be joined in an exclusive and permanent relationship as husband and wife. The marriage relationship joined by God formed the first earthly image of the Trinity. The importance of that relationship in the course of human history is second only to man's eternal relationship with God.

Why didn't God just give Adam a puppy to love and play with? A puppy was a creation of God but not his *special* creation. Eve was a special creation like Adam, but at the same time she was also the feminine version of the image of God imprinted on mankind and not just a carbon copy of lesser value than Adam. She was different but complementary to Adam in mind and body. Eve completed Adam as he completed her. Also similar to our picture of the Trinity, they were distinct in their personalities and roles but "…one in their own eternal and intense love for each other."[68] When they became one flesh, they were divinely endowed with new meaning and purpose for their lives.

How does our modern concept of equality fit into this picture? Glenn Stanton and Leon Wirth give an excellent portrayal of equality in the Christian marriage relationship.

> Eve is his equal, right by his side, figuratively and literally. She is his mate; she is human. They are both made to rule over creation together and solve each other's problem of original solitude.[69]

The feminine image of God borne by Eve is not subordinate or inferior to the masculine image that marked Adam. As noted, they were both special creations of God with different but complementary roles and purposes. But as it is within the Trinity, there is a hierarchy of authority and deference within the marriage relationship. This hierarchy is not a matter of superior or subordinate but status in family. In the Christian worldview, husbands are designated as the spiritual head of the household. Numerous scripture references confirm the spiritual headship of the husband.

> But I want you to know that the head of every man is Christ, the head of woman *is* man, and the head of Christ *is* God. [1 Corinthians 11:3. NKJV]

> Wives, submit to your own husbands, as to the Lord. For the husband is head of the wife, as also Christ is head of the church … [Ephesians 5:22-23a. NKJV]

Nothing irritates the modern liberated feminist more than this concept of submission to the authority of a husband. But if we stop here, the marital image of the divine triune relationship is incomplete for the husband also has duties and obligations within the marriage relationship.

> Husbands, likewise, dwell with *them* with understanding, giving honor to the wife, as to the weaker vessel, and as *being* heirs together of the grace of life, that your prayers may not be hindered. [1 Peter 3:7. NKJV]

> Wives, submit to your own husbands, as is fitting in the Lord. Husbands, love your wives and do not be bitter toward them. [Colossians 3:18-19. NKJV]

Here we begin to get an inkling of how marriage mirrors the Trinitarian relationship. This brings to mind Timothy Keller's divine dance but in human terms in which the marriage partners are immersed in a continuous mutual self-giving of love, intimacy, gentleness, honor, consideration, and deference.

Humanism's view of marriage and family relationships

Humanism substantially rejects the hierarchal nature of most human relationships. As a result, relational connections are more tenuous and fluid and often without long-term commitments to spouse and family. Because the humanist believes that marriage and family relationships are one of many possible social constructions, a broad and diverse array of human relationships evolves from such a worldview. In the humanistic society, these social constructions are shaped by class, gender, and ethnicity, not a non-existent God. Therefore, there can be no cultural universal of marriage and family because all viewpoints, opinions, and beliefs about social constructions are equally valid.

Humanism's broad frontal attack on the marriage and family universal is also accompanied by indirect guerrilla attacks on the institution of marriage and family as they encounter and operate within the various spheres of American life.

For over one hundred years, the traditional view of marriage and family withstood secularism's attacks that began in the mid-1800s. However, major fissures in traditional marriage and family relationships began appearing in the 1960s. Those cracks have widened to become the yawning chasm in American social structure of which marriage and family breakdown is the most significant cause. Numerous contributors to destruction of traditional marriage and the family include (1) government welfare policies that effectively separated the male from the family unit, (2) the feminist movement that sought to redefine the roles of men and women in society, (3)the homosexual agenda to redefine marriage and the meaning of family, (4) the legalization of abortion and decline of sexual mores that unhooked sexuality from marriage and family, (5) the ascendency of the humanistic worldview with the focus on self to the detriment of relationships (spouse and family), and (6) a humanistic educational system that diminishes and frustrates the role of parents in the transmission of long-held cultural values to their children.

Almost three decades ago the late Robert H. Bork wrote that radical feminism was the most destructive and fanatical movement that arose in the 1960s. "Totalitarian in spirit, it is deeply antagonistic to traditional Western culture and proposes the complete restructuring of society, morality, and human nature."[70] Here we do not speak of the huge accomplishments and advances in needed reforms such as the right to vote, equal rights in the workplace, and other equity issues. The modern feminist movement has long abandoned those issues in favor of "gender" feminism. For gender feminists, the universe revolves around the "gender perspective" in which all things are viewed in relation to the oppression of women.

> It attacks not only men but the institutions of family, it is hostile to traditional religion, it demands quotas in every field for women, and it engages in serious misrepresentation of facts. Worst of all, it inflicts great damage on persons and essential institutions in a reckless attempt to remake human beings and create a world that can never exist.[71]

Perhaps the most detrimental force to challenge the Christian understanding of marriage in the modern world is humanism's demand for so-called equality between men and women and also marriage partners. In the quest for gender equality, both the institution of marriage between a man and woman and lasting marital commitments have been reduced to a shambles. Collateral damage from this demand for equality is reflected in the statistics compiled by those who measure such matters as divorce, single-parent homes, co-habitation, out-of-wedlock births, child neglect and abuse, domestic violence, child-on-child violence, abortions, poverty, and the national decline in educational achievement. The statistics are abundant, well-documented, incontrovertible as to cause, and would be needlessly redundant to reprint here.

With little effort we can assemble the evidence needed to convict the modern feminist movement of being the "great evil" that has undermined marriage and family in America. However, the rise of the reconstituted feminist movement in the early 1960s, which has acted as the catalyst for the modern demands to change the roles of men and women, has a much longer history and is the result of a series of complex societal forces that have been in operation since the Industrial Revolution beginning in the early 1800s. During this period the American church was also negligent if not culpable in the decline of traditional marriage and family and alteration of the biblical understanding of the roles of men and women. Secular humanists used the church's negligence and acquiescence to its advantage in reconstructing the roles of men and women in the image of the modern humanist worldview.

In her book *Total Truth*, Nancy Pearcey presents an insightful analysis of the events that led to modern day feminism and the devastating changes caused by redefined roles for women *and* men. She states that the Industrial Revolution led to specialization in the work of men and women with a consequent loss of range and variety in their work. In other words, the once close cooperative association of a husband and wife in the performance of their complementary roles was reduced as men worked away from the home and therefore less integrated in family life including the male role as a parent and teacher of their children. Likewise, women became less involved in economic production. With the husband's absence, she had greater childrearing responsibilities and no longer felt a part of the real (interpreted as "worthwhile") work of society. She felt less valued and "…isolated from intellectual, economic, and political life." The roles of men and women became compartmentalized—men were devoted to matters of the public realm and women were confined to the home, the private realm.[72] This same duality of realms was happening to the church in the late 1800s and early 1900s, that is, the church was being compartmentalized and therefore isolated from all other areas of secular public life.

The response to the damage to marriage and family caused by this unnatural separation of men and women into public and private spheres came as the nation attempted to deal with the consequent societal pathologies as America reeled during the aftermath of the Civil War and subsequent excesses and failings of society in late nineteenth century. The antidote prescribed by the humanists was to reform society.

Initially, the reform movement manifested itself as the social gospel which attempted to, as Pearcey put it, "remoralize" America. The social gospel movement was focused on correcting the perceived ills of society and was headed primarily by mainstream Protestant ministers and involved significant support from women.[73] Those Protestant ministers emphasized social justice over perfecting the inner man, and the relationship of Christians to others in society." They also embraced the concept of the inherent perfectibility of man, and their worldview was much closer to those of the social Darwinists than to the fundamental biblical doctrines of the Baptists and traditional Methodists. The social gospel movement was a big tent that included many secularists and other social Darwinists who quickly marginalized and eventually eliminated any hint of Christian core beliefs and teachings the movement may once have had.[74]

One may ask what the remainder of America churches was during the social gospel era. Many of these churches rightly feared the mainline church's social gospel. They saw the social gospel as being close to a gospel of "salvation by works" and a tool to accomplish left-wing social reform. But their fears, however justified, led to an abandonment of their biblical role in charitable works to that of government. Because of a general loss of cultural authority to the secular humanists and doctrinal failings of the liberal church, the conservative and evangelical churches developed a "ghetto mentality," which wrongly held society at arm's length while burying themselves in prayer, Bible study, converting the lost, and personal morality and holiness. But in doing so, they also abandoned their responsibility to society to be the salt of the earth as commanded by Christ in Matthew 5:13. Because the conservative and evangelical churches withdrew from cultural engagement, its inherent saltiness could no longer "…flavor the nation's culture, arts, music, movies, laws, and politics…and preserve the nation from the disastrous consequences of immorality."[75]

Because of the liberal church's doctrinal failure by embracing the humanistic worldview of the perfectibility of man and the conservative evangelical church's "ghetto-mentality" and abandonment of the public arena, the task of reforming society was left to the secular social Darwinists. Schweikart and Allen captured the mindset of that era.

> Secularist reformers continued the quest for perfectionism with something like a religious zeal. They wielded great influence in the first decade of the new century. By 1912, progressives found adherents in both political parties and had substantial support from women, who supported health and safety laws and prohibition and temperance legislation. In turn, woman suffrage became a centerpiece of all Progressive reform.[76]

Many of these early reforms efforts were not hostile to doctrines and concerns of biblical Christianity. In fact, most have been important *concerns* of the Christian church since the time of Christ. But because of the absence of a visible, vocal, and doctrinally-sound church in culture and the various spheres of America life, many of the secularist-humanist *solutions* proposed and adopted during the first half of the twentieth century were anti-marriage and anti-family. Although these humanistic solutions were based on a false worldview and failed from their inception, those solutions would be vastly expanded and implemented with a vengeance as the humanistic worldview captured much of the leadership of the institutions of American life beginning in the 1960s.

The angry, sign-wielding suffragette of the early 1900s confronted by the taunts of a hostile crowd is often portrayed as the image of the modern feminist. However, many of those early feminists limited their efforts to well-justified and biblically sound causes. But there were notable exceptions during that era who became the matriarchs of the liberal feminists of the 1960s that were concerned about supposed injustices that existed *subsequent to a redefinition of the roles of men and women in society*. It is when we look at the redefinition of those roles and the demands to correct the perceived injustices that we see the significant damage that has been inflicted upon the traditional understanding of marriage and family.

Although the feminist movement declined in the years following World War II, a book written in 1963 by Betty Friedan would provide the spark that led to the rebirth of the women's movement in the 1960s. In *The Feminine Mystique*, Friedan wrote about "the problem that has no name," the supposed alienation and meaninglessness experienced by the typical housewife.[77]

Three years later while meeting with a group of like-minded women, the National Organization of Women (NOW) was founded. The stated purpose that came out of those meetings was unmistakably clear in its mission to *fundamentally change the role of women in American Society*.

> NOW is dedicated to the proposition that women…must have the chance to develop their *fullest human potential*…it is no longer either necessary or possible for women to devote the greater part of their lives to child-rearing; yet childbearing and rearing, which continues to be a most important part of most women's lives—still is used to justify barring women from equal professional and economic participation and advance. We do not accept the traditional assumption that a woman has to choose between marriage and motherhood, on the one hand, and serious participation in industry or the professions on the other. True *equality of opportunity and freedom of choice* for women requires such practical, and possible innovations as a nationwide network of child care centers, which will make it unnecessary for women to retire completely form society until their children are grown…We reject the assumptions that a man must carry the sole burden of supporting himself, his wife, and family, and that a woman is automatically entitled to lifelong support by a

man upon her marriage, or that marriage, home and family are primarily woman's world and responsibility—hers, to dominate—his to support...We will seek to open a *reexamination of laws and mores governing marriage and divorce*...We are similarly opposed to all policies and practices—in church, state, college, factory, or office—which, in the guise of protectiveness, not only deny opportunities but also foster in women self-denigration, dependence, and evasion of responsibility, undermine their confidence in their own abilities and foster contempt for women.[78] [emphasis added]

Personally written by Friedan, the NOW Statement of Purpose carries the trademark language of the humanistic worldview. This is borne out by the fact that not only was Friedan a signor of the 1973 *Humanist Manifesto II*, she was named Humanist of the Year in 1975.

How can one know which worldview presents the true picture of the marriage relationship and the roles men and women are to have? Are marriage and family and the biblical roles of men and women divinely fixed by God, or are they merely social constructions to meet the whims of mankind in accordance with humanist orthodoxy? One source for truth when constructing one's worldview is anthropology—the study of man and how he has lived in all ages and places. Although anthropologists often attempt to interpret the facts gathered by their research, their primary task is fact-gathering. And the facts with regard to the traditional institution of marriage and family speak for themselves.

Renowned anthropologist Margaret Mead in her book *Male and Female*, published in 1949, wrote:

When we survey all known human societies, we find everywhere some form of the family, some set of permanent arrangements by which males assist females in caring for children while they are young...In every known human society, everywhere in the world, the young male learns that when he grows up, one of the things he must do in order to be a full member of society is to provide food for some female and her young...Every known human society rests firmly on the learned nurturing behavior of men.[79]

Yale anthropologist George Peter Murdock defined and explained marriage and family across cultures in his landmark book

Social Structure, published the same year as Mead's book. He described the nuclear family as consisting of a married man and woman and their children. Stanton and Wirth summarized Murdock's explanation of the nuclear family, "...the term 'nuclear family' is not a moral, traditionalist, or even Western cultural term, but a universal, anthropological one describing the fundamental and most irreducible building block of any society."[80]

As one reflects on how humans have organized themselves over time, there is and has been a great diversity of societal forms in different cultures and periods of history. However, underlying this variety is a structured order or arrangement that reflects the "creational givens." One of these creational givens is the universal structure of marriage and family. And the family structure consisting of "...a father, mother and children living together in bonds of committed caring is not an arbitrary happenstance; nor is it mere convention that can be dismissed when it has outlived its usefulness." This ordered family structure is a part of the human constitution and is ingrained in man's nature in all of its facets—biological, emotional, social and moral. The family structure may come in many varieties and differences, but all must reside within a set of definite boundaries, that is, lines that cannot be crossed without being in opposition to the universal and unchanging meaning of family.[81]

This ordered family structure is the creation of God and is described in Genesis 1:27. "God created man in his own image...male and female he created them..." The characters and roles of the male and female are distinct, but both are created in His image. Therefore, the roles of husband and wife and father and mother (monogamous married couple living with their children) are not societal constructs from which they are to be liberated. True human fulfillment is attained when men and women are faithful to the foundational principles of the God-created marriage and family structure. The outward fabric of the family may vary markedly in various cultures and societies down through the ages, but the divinely ordered family structure is intrinsically a part of the fundamental identity of the family in every society and for all time.[82] This ordered family structure is one of those universals, norms, eternal truths, or permanent things that are imbedded in the foundation of God's creation. Cultures and societies cannot violate this ordered structure with impunity and escape eventual destruction.

It is not necessary to adhere to the Judeo-Christian worldview to recognize that marriage is a cultural universal. Kay S. Hymowitz wrote *Marriage and Caste in America* in which describes the post-marital age of separate and unequal families. Ms. Hymowitz does not speak from religious conviction and is a self-described agnostic. However, she recognizes that marriage is a "human universal" which "exists in every known society, no matter how poor or rich..." She describes a widening gap in American social structure in which family breakdown is the driving force behind poverty and other ills of modern society in America. She states, "...there is no way to attack these worrisome economic trends without tackling culture—the system of beliefs, values, and practices that help us define and live a good life."[83] When Hymowitz links marriage and family breakdown to society's flawed "beliefs, values, and practices," she is effectively linking the human universal of marriage with certain distinct and unchangeable roles for men and women. In other words, at some fundamental level the roles of men and women are *not interchangeable and cannot be equalized through homogenization by whimsical man.*

While it is nice to have the facts as presented by sociologists and anthropologists on one's side, the ultimate test of a worldview is in the *operation* of those worldviews in the lives of men and women. What has mankind found that works best with regard to marriage, family, and the roles of men and women? In their superb book *The Case for Marriage*, Linda Waite and Maggie Gallagher wrote,

> As a species, we have developed social institutions over eons to get the most out of these creatures that we are. The family, focused around the married couple, forms the keystone of these universal social institutions." As the traditional Protestant marriage ceremony puts it: "To have and to hold from this day forward, for better, for worse for richer or poorer, in sickness and in health, to love and to cherish, till death do us part."...
>
> Decades of social-science research have confirmed the deepest intuitions of the human heart: As frightening, exhilarating, and improbable as this wild vow of constancy may seem, there is no substitute. When love seeks permanence, a safe home for children who long for both parents, when men and women look for someone they can count on, there are no substitutes. The word for what we mean is *marriage*.[84] (emphasis in original)

Here we repeat the admonition given at the beginning of this chapter. When we speak of marriage and family relationships, we must also speak of the roles of men and women. It is more than a symbiotic relationship; they are inseparable. One cannot be fully understood without an understanding of the other. To injure one is to injure the other.

In their tampering with the universal roles of men and women to achieve radical egalitarianism's gender equality through the creation of man-made social, political, and economic rights and privileges, humanists have wreaked havoc on the human universal of marriage and family.

8

Equality and Church-State Relationship

As with the God-man and marriage-family relationships, the views of Christianity and humanism are markedly different with regard to the respective purposes, roles, and relational interactions of church and state.

The followers of Christ form the body of Christ and are the universal Church. Both the body of Christ and the institutional face of the church have certain roles, responsibilities, and limitations as they interact with the state. Likewise, government was instituted by God and has certain purposes and roles distinct from but complementary to the church.

In the humanist worldview there is no God, and any belief in God is compartmentalized as religion which has no role in the affairs of the state and the various institutions of public life. It is the virtual separation of the spiritual and the secular into dual realms in modern America that has become the vortex of the culture wars. In this war of worldviews, humanists attempt to marginalize and subordinate the church's influence in society to that of state-mandated egalitarianism. And it is egalitarianism, (a state-defined and state-imposed equality) that is the subject of this book. The role which equality occupies in the Christian and humanist perceptions of church-state relationships is radically different. Before we examine equality's role, we must have a deeper understanding of those worldviews with regard to church and state.

The Christian view of church-state relationships

What is the role of the state and where does it obtain its authority? The biblical view is that God created the state to *restrain evil* in this world (which is also a role of family and the church) and to *promote a just social order* (not to be confused with social justice as defined by humanism). Here we see that government's role is not meant to be a mere pawn subservient to the will of the people.[85] When creating the American Republic, the Founders had a keen understanding of the fallen nature of man and were justly wary of the unrestrained "will of the people." As a result, they took great pains to build restraints and safeguards into the new nation's structure of governance.

Why did God need civil government to restrain evil? Weren't the universal truths evident in His creation and the biblical revelation sufficient to put the brakes on sin? God knew the inherent sin-nature of fallen man and that many would reject His authority. He foresaw the need for a commonly held authority to restrain both His followers and those that rebelled against his authority. This authority placed limits and imposed guidelines on human behavior regarding earthly matters in this temporal world. The state was not created to rehabilitate a broken world nor has it the power to do so. The state is limited to promoting "...the good of the community in its temporal concerns, the protection of life and property, and the preservation of peace and order." The solutions for mankind's travail must come from the church, but at the same time the church must not infringe upon these legitimate roles of government through attempts to establish the kingdom of God upon this earth through civil authority (i.e., a theocracy). [86]

In addition to its task of restraining evil through limitations on human behavior, it also has the positive role of promoting a *just* social order. Here we return to our earlier definition of justice. The ideals of fairness, impartiality, and right action are the stuff of justice, "...the principle or process by which every man and woman in society are accorded the things that are rightfully their own: their lives, their dignity, their property, their station in life." Again we must note that *justice* is not the same as *law* but is of a higher order and by its nature involves morality. Justice prevails when men's actions and courts of law mirror justice's ethical standards.[87]

Because the state is a legitimate creation of God, the Christian has certain obligations to the state. The Apostle Paul defined this role in his letter to the Roman church.

> Let every soul be subject to the governing authorities. For there is no authority except from God, and the authorities that exist are appointed by God. Therefore whoever resists the authority resists the ordinance of God, and those who resist will bring judgment on themselves. For rulers are not a terror to good works, but to evil. Do you want to be unafraid of the authority? Do what is good, and you will have praise from the same. For he is God's minister to you for good. But if you do evil, be afraid; for he does not bear the sword in vain; for he is God's minister, an avenger to *execute* wrath on him who practices evil. Therefore *you* must be subject, not only because of wrath but also for conscience' sake. [Romans 13:1-5. NKJV]

This can be a difficult passage for many Christians to understand and accept in the face of hostile government authorities. Our difficulties may be lessened as we examine and understand key phrases in Paul's instruction: *For there is no authority except from God, and those that exist have been instituted by God*, and *Rulers are not a terror to good conduct*. Here we must distinguish between those who rule with and without authority. Secondly, we know that certain rulers are a terror to good conduct.

Dietrich Bonhoeffer was a brilliant German theologian, pastor, and opponent of the Nazi regime since its beginning in 1933. In April 1945, during the closing days of World War II, he was hanged on a Nazi gallows upon the personal order of Adolf Hitler. He went to his death with a very definite understanding of the role of the church in society. Bonhoeffer believed that God instituted government for the preservation of order and the establishment of laws that define that order. He also firmly believed the church plays a vital role in helping the state be the state by continually asking if the state's actions can be justified as a legitimate fulfillment of its role. Put another way, the church must ask if the actions of the state promote law and order or lead to lawlessness and disorder. If the state fails to fulfill its role, the church's role is to draw the state's attention to its failure. Likewise, if the state creates an atmosphere of "excessive law and order," the church must also remind the state of its proper role. Excessive law and order becomes evident when the state's power develops "…to such an extent that it deprives Christian preaching and Christian faith…of their rights."[88]

When the church draws attention to the state's failures and/or over-reach of its proper role, the church is not interfering or dictating to the state but fulfilling its role as salt and light to the world (See: Matthew 5:13-14). Bonhoeffer strongly denied that the church was an instrument of the state and therefore subject to state authority. Rather, the church was set apart from the state, and the church's roles and purposes were derived from God's authority. When the state seeks to impose its authority on the church in contradiction to the state's God-ordained purpose and role, the state oversteps the boundaries of its *legitimate* authority.[89]

What should be the church's response be to a state that oversteps its legitimate authority? Bonhoeffer believes that the church should continue its mission of informing and exhorting the state to fulfill only the proper role of government. Secondly, the church should aid all victims (both Christian and non-Christian) of the state due to the abandonment and/or excesses of its legitimate authority. Bonhoeffer also said that a third step may be necessary. The church must

> …not just bandage the victims under the wheel…but a stick must be jammed into the spokes of the wheel to stop the vehicle. It is sometimes not enough to help those crushed by the evil actions of a state; at some point the church must directly take action against the state to stop it from perpetrating evil.[90]

However, Bonhoeffer cautioned that the stick in the spokes of the wheel of state is justified *only* if the church's very existence is threatened by the state *and* the state is no longer a state as designed by God.[91] Here we must distinguish between bad government and rulers without legitimate authority over the state. Christians must still be subject to bad governments and its laws and regulations even when they disagree with them. However, when rulers and their laws and regulations threaten the continued existence of the Christian faith and require Christians to violate their beliefs, the state has forfeited any legitimate authority which it may have had.

Here we have clarification to the words of Paul. The church is not obligated to obey the state when the state threatens the very existence of the church. Those rulers either never had legitimate authority or it was withdrawn by God. And without legitimate authority, those rulers can be a terror to good conduct. It is nonsensical to believe that such rulers retain *legitimate* authority and must be mindlessly obeyed because of a misunderstanding of the meaning of Romans 13:1-5. The rejection of illegitimate civil authorities for cause is found in both the Old and New Testaments.

The authority of King Saul was withdrawn when he presumed to usurp the authority the prophet Samuel by offering the burnt offering in Samuel's absence. When Samuel was told of Saul's disobedience to God's commandment, he said to Saul, "…You have done foolishly…But now your kingdom shall not continue…" [1 Samuel 13:13a, 14a. NKJV] Although Saul retained his power for many years, his legitimate authority was ended upon Samuel's pronouncement.

Because the Romans saw value in all religions, they built the Pantheon in Rome to honor all gods. With the birth of the early church and its dispersion throughout the Roman Empire, the Christian God was also welcomed if only the His followers would compromise their beliefs and give some tribute and deference to Roman gods.[92] But those early Christians served a jealous God and would not obey the Roman authorities and unequivocally held to His commandment, "You shall have no other gods before Me." [Exodus 20:3. NKJV] Because of their disobedience to Roman authority, the Apostle Paul and thousands of Christians in the early church were slain in the Roman Coliseum and jails.

In the biblical worldview, the spheres of church and state are not competitors, but each has an important and complementary purpose and role to play in the lives of its citizens. Alexis de Tocqueville eloquently described the symbiotic relationship between church and state that still existed when he wrote of it over four decades after the founding of the American Republic.

> On my arrival in the United States, it was the religious atmosphere which first struck me. As I extended my stay, I could observe the *political consequences* which flowed from this novel situation.
>
> In France I had seen the spirit of religion moving in the opposite direction to that of the spirit of freedom. In America, I found them intimately linked together in *joint reign* over the same land.[93] [emphasis added]

Tocqueville attributed the peaceful influence exercised by religion over the nation to separation of church and state.[94] Unlike the modernists' separation of church and state, Tocqueville's separation was a separation of the spheres of power and *not a separation of government from ethics and moral guidance supplied by the moral suasion of Christianity*. The very foundation of the cultural concept is unity that assumes a general commonality of thought and action. In other words, a nation must be informed by ethics and moral guidance. John Quincy Adams unequivocally identified America's source for its ethics and moral guidance.

> The highest glory of the American Revolution was this; it connected in one indissoluble bond the principles of civil government with the principles of Christianity... From the day of the Declaration...they (the American people), were bound by the laws of God, which they all, and by the laws of their Gospel, which they nearly all, acknowledge as the rules of conduct."[95]

The Founders encouraged the church's ethical and moral influence upon government, and for one hundred fifty years the church played a vital role in helping the state be the state by continually asking if the state's actions were justified as a legitimate fulfillment of its role.

Much has been said about the roles of the church and state from the perspective of the Christian worldview. But what of equality? Even before the creation of the state, it was in His creation of man that God revealed the divine truth about human equality. "And He has made from one blood every nation of men to dwell on all the face of the earth, and has determined their pre-appointed times and the boundaries of their dwellings." [Acts 17:26. NKJV] Luke's account in the Acts of the Apostles speaks of God's creation of all peoples with *one blood* which implies that we should treat each of God's special creations with dignity, kindness, patience, and respect that pertains to a family member with a blood relationship.

If Paul's words are an example for the church, the church in its role to inform and motivate the state in the area of ethics and moral guidance should admonish the state to follow this standard of human equality in the civil arena for both Christians and non-Christians.

Humanism's view of church-state relationships

In his book *The Road to Serfdom*, F. A. Hayek begins his chapter titled "The Great Utopia" with a quote from Johann Hölderlin.

> What has always made the state a hell on earth has been precisely that man has tried to make it his heaven.[96]

In *Humanist Manifestos I and II*, one finds the architectural plans by which man attempted to create his heaven on earth through the machinations of a humanistic state but which over time has produced only an earthly hell.

> We believe, however, that traditional dogmatic or *authoritarian* religions that place revelation, God, ritual, or creed above human needs and experience do a disservice to the human species. Any account of nature should pass the tests of scientific evidence; in our judgment, the dogmas and myths of traditional religion do not do so.
>
> …we can discover no divine purpose or providence for the human species…No deity will save; we must save ourselves.
>
> …Promises of immortal salvation or fear of eternal damnation are both illusory and harmful. They distract from present concerns, from self-actualization, and from rectifying social injustices.
>
> The separation of church and state and the separation of ideology and state are imperatives.[97]

In just a few sentences we see humanism's blithe dismissal of religion and the church in the affairs of state. In the humanist worldview, religion and the church shall have no authority to inform or motivate culture. Because of the ascension of the humanistic worldview in the various spheres of society, the assault on the church has intensified and its voice and authority in society is being significantly ridiculed, marginalized, and ultimately displaced.

In discussing the relationship of church and state from the Christian perspective, we saw a triadic relational pattern between God, the church, and state with God as the source of authority. In the humanist worldview, the relational pattern is between natural man and the state with the state holding ultimate authority. The state derives its authority from the man-made philosophy of humanism and its depiction of the nature of man and his origins, purpose, and destiny. The state is charged with the task of furthering the tenets of the humanistic faith: There is no God. Man is the product of a long evolutionary development which occurred by chance. Man's purpose is to achieve happiness in this life through self-actualization. Individual efforts at happiness are superseded only by the goals of a society which seeks the greater good for all mankind as defined by that society's self-appointed elites.

We have previously stated that, in the Christian worldview, the state does not play a role in redeeming society. However, humanism proposes to do that very thing. This following describes the scenario in which man proposes to "redeem society." Humanism professes that man is not fallen and subject to damnation but must save himself. Because man is basically good, he will become progressively better and better through the advancement of education, science, and reason. Because all men are born equal, societal problems must arise from man's faulty or corrupt institutions that create inequalities. Mankind will flourish as man's institutions are reformed or eliminated and replaced with better institutions to eliminate these inequalities. It is the state's role to organize and operate a humanist society so that human progress will not be impeded in achieving the removal of any inequalities among humankind. In its quest for human equality, the state must place special emphasis on social, political, and economic rights and privileges. The state's tools for accomplishing its egalitarian mission are laws, rulings, regulations, decrees, policies, and directives, and neither constitutional nor legislative interference will be tolerated.

In the humanistic worldview, the laws of the state arise from the *needs and experiences* of mankind as opposed to the arbitrary sanctions of God, religion, revelation, ritual, or creed. Unhooked from the anchor of eternal truth, fickle man's needs and experiences are continually changing. So too must the state's relativistic laws change which also prompts continually changing definitions of order, justice, and freedom which it imposes on society. The end result is that the tail (laws) is wagging the dog (order, justice, and freedom).

The American Republic upon which the nation was founded rested on the biblical worldview of the Founders and was reflected in the crafting of the Constitution. Fundamental to this form of government were Constitutional limitations placed upon the powers of the state.

America was to be a nation ruled by laws created by the elected representatives of its citizenry. It was intended that those laws must always fit within Constitutional boundaries as fixed by the Founders and subsequent Amendments thereto. Because America is a nation ruled by law, the implication is that governmental authority (power) is limited and may only be exercised in accordance with written laws adopted through an established procedure.[98]

The Founders were adamant that the Constitution should be an unchanging guide by which to measure the constitutionality of the laws of the land. In other words, the original intent of the Founders in writing the Constitution and its Amendments was to guide the courts in their work of interpreting the Constitution. Thomas Jefferson's admonishment to Supreme Court Justice William Johnson stated that,

> On every question of construction, carry ourselves back to the time when the Constitution was adopted, recollect the spirit manifested in the debates, and instead of trying what meaning may be squeezed out of the text, or invented against it, conform to the probable one in which it was passed.[99]

Joseph Story was the leading Constitutional scholar of the nineteenth century and in 1833 wrote in *Commentaries on the Constitution* that the Constitution "…was to be understood in terms of its plain, commonsense meaning" and must not be changed by the caprice of men.

> The reader must not expect to find in these pages any novel construction of the Constitution. I have not the ambition to be the author of any new plan of interpreting the theory of the Constitution, or enlarging or narrowing its powers, by ingenious subtleties and learned doubts…"[100]

Until the mid-twentieth century, the Founders' original intent was the courts' coin of the realm in interpreting the Constitution. However, efforts at abandonment of original intent began much earlier when Christopher Columbus Langdell became president of Harvard Law School in 1870. Langdell developed the theory of *legal positivism* which was adopted and applied by other leading lawyers and jurists that followed him including Supreme Court Justice Oliver Wendell Holmes. Under the theory of legal positivism, there are no objective, God-given standards of law. Therefore, the author of law must be man because the state says it is the law and backs it up by force. Since man and society evolve, so too must law evolve as well. Judicial decisions guide the evolution of the law (i.e., judges make law). Therefore, the decisions of the judges become the source of the law.[101]

In 1914, Woodrow Wilson championed legal positivism while disparaging the original intent of the Founders in interpreting the Constitution.

> And they [the authors of the Constitution] constructed a government...to display the laws of Nature...The government was to exist and move by virtue of the efficacy of "checks and balances." The trouble with this theory is that government is not a machine, but a living thing. It falls not under the theory of the universe, but under the theory of organic life. It is accountable to Darwin...Government is not a body of blind forces; it is a body of men...Living political constitutions must be Darwinian in structure and in practice. Society is a living organism and must obey the laws of Life, not of mechanics, it must develop. All that progressives ask or desire is permission—in an era when "development," "evolution," is the scientific word—to interpret the Constitution according to the Darwinian principle; all they ask is recognition of the fact that a nation is a living thing and not a machine.[102]

Wilson's profoundly humanistic understanding of man is based on the Darwinian belief that man is basically good and ever progressing. Because men and society evolve, so must their constitutions and laws. Therefore, Wilson jettison's the Founders' concern for the universal wickedness of fallen man and thereafter dispenses with the need for those pesky "checks and balances" so important to the Founders.

Under the protection of legal positivism, unelected judges and elected or appointed officials and bureaucrats abuse their authority through creation of unjust laws and supporting court decisions which reach beyond the original intent of the Founders and ignore the checks and balances inherent in the Constitution. This abuse of power has increased significantly during the last eight decades as a result of the increasing rejection of the biblical worldview and the adoption of a humanistic, secular worldview by many of the leaders of American institutions and especially leaders of government and related bureaucracies.[103] The consequences of the implementation of unjust laws and supporting court decisions are the creation of a new social order founded on a false worldview, perversion of the true meaning of justice, and significant limitations of freedom.

The retreat from the biblical worldview as the basis for our laws and policy making began accelerating in the 1930s. Concurrently, there also began a vast increase in the scope and authority of bureaucratic government over all other spheres of American social order in a manner not intended by the Founders or God's design for that social order. Such governmental abuse of its power occurs when the state usurps the power, authority, and roles of other spheres of the social structure designed by God. Here we speak of the individual, family, church, labor, community, and relationship between man and God. This intrusion of the state into all spheres of society has become so powerful, pervasive, and complex, that even the most ardent socialist cannot deny it.[104]

In the humanists' efforts to create a new social order centered on the great goddess of Equality, they have instituted laws that conflict with man's true nature and his divine purpose. These new laws are designed to make possible the state's establishment of a new heaven on earth. To enter this new heaven, man need only to accept the new laws and surrender his old notions of order, justice, and freedom in exchange for new ones codified and blessed by the goddess of Equality who reigns over the new heaven. When man discovers the new heaven over which the goddess of Equality rules is in reality an earthly hell, he will curse his masters, but it will be too late to break the chains of his bondage.

9

Equality and Man-Community Relationships

In this chapter we examine man's nature as it relates to the concepts of *fraternity* versus *equality* which is a subset of the more comprehensive theme of human relationships discussed in later chapters.

According to Simone Weil, one of the greatest needs of the human soul is *rootedness*. One has roots "…by virtue of his real, active, and natural participation in the life of a community, which preserves in living shape certain particular treasures of the past and certain particular expectations for the future."[105] Put another way, the loss of roots or rootlessness can be said to be a *loss of center* or *an absence of fixed reference points*. Without such, a person drifts or wanders through life in a meaningless existence devoid of connectedness or orientation. With regard to human relationships, these sentiments as to the importance of connectedness and orientation carry significant implications for the concepts of fraternity and equality. Because of differences in their inherent natures, there is a potential for tension and hostility between fraternity and equality which has been greatly magnified by the culture wars between the opposing worldviews of Christianity and humanism.

We begin with equality. Much like democracy, equality has become a modern icon to be worshiped without question, an end rather than a means. And also like democracy, equality can become a corrupt and arbitrary tyrant that enslaves, bullies, and brutalizes the citizens over whom it holds sway. Such is happening in twenty-first century America.

Modern democratic ideas of human equality were advanced by French Enlightenment philosophies of human goodness and perfectibility of man that sprang fully formed from the humanistic worldview. For what men are comes from experience. Therefore, men are equal at birth, and differences and inequalities arise due to environment. The solution is education that will result in an ideal democratic society.[106] The humanistic concept of equality elevated the status of the individual above community as codified by *Humanist Manifesto II* in 1973.

> The *preciousness and dignity of the individual person* is a central humanist value. Individuals should be encouraged to realize their own creative talents and desires. We reject all religious, ideological, or moral codes that denigrate the individual, suppress freedom, dull intellect, and dehumanize personality. We believe in a maximum individual autonomy consonant with social responsibility. Although science can account for the

> cause of behavior, the possibilities of individual *freedom of choice* exist in human life and should be increased. In the area of sexuality, we believe that intolerant attitudes, often cultivated by orthodox religions and puritanical cultures, unduly repress sexual conduct. The right to birth control, abortion, and divorce should be recognized…The many varieties of sexual exploration should not in themselves be considered "evil".[107] [emphasis in original]

This undefined egalitarianism is the most sinister idea to breakdown society. Egalitarianism is a sworn enemy of hierarchy. Also, if society means order, then humanistic egalitarianism is a disordering concept with regard to human relationships in a society. It imposes injustice where it pretends redress for injustice. It frustrates and undermines natural social groupings. It creates an overflowing "reservoir of poisonous envy" from which flow rivers of hostility, resentment, and suspicion.[108]

Wilfred McClay wrote, "…we shape our relationships, but we are more fundamentally shaped by the need for them, and we cannot understand ourselves without reference to them…we are made by, through, and for relationship with one another."[109] One of the fundamental needs of mankind is to dwell together, in other words, a need for relationships. For the Christian, the importance of human relationships is a reflection of the Trinitarian relationship, a picture of His fundamental being. God's being is shown by the Father-Son relationship and the relationship of Christ with the Church of which He is the head and His followers are the body. For mankind, the divine relational pattern is present in various entities—marriage, family, community, nations, and the Kingdom of God.

These image-of-God relationships imply fraternity and are other-directed whereas equality is self-directed and tends to egotism. Richard Weaver superbly captures the importance of fraternity as opposed to equality in achieving a well-ordered society.

> The comity of peoples in groups large or small rests not upon this chimerical notion of equality but upon fraternity, a concept which long antedates it (equality) in history because it (fraternity) goes immeasurably deeper in human sentiment. The ancient feeling of brotherhood carries obligations of which equality knows nothing…It places people in a network of sentiment, not of rights—that *hortus siccus* (dry garden) of modern vainglory.[110] [emphasis in original]

From this brief examination of the nature of fraternity/brotherhood versus humanism's equality, we have formed our hypothesis. Now, we must examine that hypothesis in the laboratory of life. We do so by surveying the most divisive issue in our nation's history, that of slavery and the subsequent 150-year effort to remove the chasm of hostility between the races.

The humanistic pursuit of equality and the growing racial division in America

There are occasions when the chains of injustice may be broken only by the hammer of the state. However, if the goal is restoration of community and brotherhood, i.e., *fraternity*, then by default restoration must ultimately be a matter of the heart. Too often the hammer of state is chosen over the heart and forced equality becomes an end rather than the means to fraternity. History and human nature have much to say about which worldview works and which does not.

The motivation and drive for ending slavery came from the early Americans who held the biblical worldview and recognized the wrongness of slavery. It was a matter of right versus wrong, not a matter of "rights" or equality. The abolitionists were primarily Christians who believed in the brotherhood of man and understood that, as the Apostle Paul said, we were all created of one blood. And this opposition to slavery in America began in 1671 by Quaker George Fox and later by William Penn and John Woolman and their followers, a little more than a half century after the first European settlers arrived on the continent.[111]

History has proven that the years following protracted wars are generally periods of significant moral decline. This was true of the remaining years of the eighteenth century following the Revolutionary War (1776-1781). All Protestant denominations began to feel the effects of the war years, especially during the last decade of the century. However, the last decade of the eighteenth century saw many isolated spiritual rumblings among the faithful that culminated in the Second Great Awakening of the early 1800s. The Second Great Awakening restored a considerable measure of morality to America and initiated other civilizing influences on the young nation including popular education, Bible Societies, Sunday schools, the modern missionary movement, and ultimately sowed and nurtured the seeds that led to the abolition of slavery. And out of this spiritual awakening came a renewed awareness of the necessity of ending the institution of slavery which resulted in the formation of many new anti-slavery societies. By 1830, the issue of slavery divided most churches, and abolition of slavery had become the burning moral issue of the century because slavery "…degraded man and his morals…cursed both the white and black races…became the enemy both of morality and religion." The flames of this burning moral issue were fanned by Charles Finney and the great revivals which began in 1824. Hundreds of thousands of Finney's converts championed the causes of the Kingdom of God including education, women's rights, and temperance. But the greatest of Finney's Christian social movements was the crusade for the abolition of slavery. Through Finney and his seventy anti-slavery evangelists, the message was carried throughout the nation. Because of Finney and other abolitionists, the decade of the 1830s transformed the American mind with regard to the issue of slavery.[112]

The three decades 1830-1860 proved to be exceptionally tumultuous and threatened the survival of the union. However, there was a providential third Awakening that occurred just prior to the Civil War and prepared the nation to endure and survive the coming Civil War and its tragic aftermath.

The Revival of 1857-1858 influenced many young men who would later spark several large and widespread revivals in both Union and Confederate armies between 1862 and 1865. Conversions during the war were estimated to be between 100,000 and 200,000 among Union troops and as many as 150,000 in the Confederate Army.[113] One may ask how this can be—brothers fighting and killing each other while both called on the same God for protection and to save their immortal souls. To answer, we must remember that slavery was an institutional cancer on the national body. Regardless of slavery's origins and protectors, it was slavery that was being cut from the body, not the Southern soldier and citizen. God was just as concerned for the individual Southerner as he was for those in the North.

As previously stated, breaking the chains of injustice sometimes requires the hammer of state in the cause of brotherhood and fraternity. The Civil War cost 600,000 lives and billions of dollars, and the nation was tragically divided with little thoughts of brotherhood. The war and the years following the draconian Reconstruction Act of 1867 left the South lying prostrate and ravaged. Called the Tragic Era, Sherwood Eddy paints a picture of the dozen years of life in the South following the Civil War.

> Often with flagrant disregard of civil liberties, Southern officials, courts, customs, and organizations were removed or swept away, and a government by Northern Carpetbaggers and Negroes was substituted under military tribunals. A Northern army of occupation of twenty thousand was aided by an irritating force of colored militia...The state administrations under Northern carpetbaggers were extravagant, corrupt, and vulgar. The state treasuries were systematically looted...The majority of the legislature and most of the

important officers were held by Negroes and many of the rest were rascally whites from the North, or unsavory characters from the South. Taxes were levied by the Negroes, of whom 80 percent were illiterate, and were paid by the disfranchised whites…the future of the Negro was sadly prejudiced by these disreputable adventures in self-government.[114]

Efforts to abolish slavery in America began as a result of the moral suasion of Christian people who saw slavery as morally unacceptable within the biblical worldview. Yet, as we have seen, the post-war *product* of the hammer of state that broke the chains of injustice was *absent Christian principles and brotherhood* and therefore was anything but moral. Thus, we must ask how it was possible for the nation to survive the cataclysmic events of the Civil War and subsequent Tragic Era in the midst of moral degradation and dashed hopes for brotherhood and unity. Once again we must look for the answer in the actions of Christians who provided the motivation and drive to end slavery based on their biblical belief in the brotherhood of man. And after the war it was the individual Christian who remained faithful and eventually restored a measure of unity and brotherhood to a society on the brink of disintegration.

In spite of the rampant corruption and immorality that plagued both the North and South for decades after the Civil war, many of the faithful Civil War veterans who embraced Christianity during the revivals on both sides of the conflict returned to their homes with their religious fervor intact, filled the pews, spurred post-war revivals (particularly in the South), and brought healing to the nation.[115] Without this unifying force of Christianity and individual Christians who *sheltered the flame of brotherhood*, the healing would have been stillborn which could have easily and likely led to a permanent balkanization of much of the South.

Almost one hundred years after the beginning of the Civil War, another movement was in progress to further efforts to lessen the chasm between the races. Compared to all prior progress in advancement of racial equality since the Civil War, the twenty year period between the beginning of World War II and 1960 was unmatched. There was significant progress in the 1940s and 1950s in moving toward the American ideals with regard to discrimination and racism.

The attitudes of Americans about race, minorities, ethnic groups, and discrimination in general were changing for the better, and the change of attitudes was followed by action. It was at the beginning of the decade of the 1960s that Martin Luther King, Jr. mounted the national stage with a message of brotherhood and hope. King drew Americans toward the goal of racial equality, harmony, and brotherhood with the high ideals espoused his eloquent "Letter from the Birmingham Jail" on April 16, 1963, and in his "I Have a Dream" speech four months later in Washington, D.C.[116] King called segregation morally wrong and sinful. And it was not the fleeting and formless morality of humanists. King espoused the biblical moral code that flowed from the teachings of Jesus Christ which he made abundantly evident in his closing paragraph of his letter from the Birmingham to his fellow clergymen.

> I hope this letter finds you strong in the faith. I also hope that circumstances will soon make it possible for me to meet each of you, not as an integrationist or a civil rights leader, but as a fellow clergyman and a Christian brother. Let us all hope that the dark clouds of racial prejudice will soon pass away and the deep fog of misunderstanding will be lifted from our fear-drenched communities and in some not too distant tomorrow the radiant stars of *love and brotherhood* will shine over our great nation with all their scintillating beauty. Yours for the cause of Peace and *Brotherhood*.[117] [emphasis added]

King recognized that the goal of equality could only be achieved under the greater goal of racial harmony and brotherhood through recognition and observance of those norms flowing from the Judeo-Christian tradition. Whatever King's hopes for racial harmony and brotherhood may have been, those hopes ended with an assassin's bullet on April 4, 1968. However, many within and without the civil rights movement wanted nothing to do with King's non-violent methods or his reliance on the norms of Judeo-Christian tradition in the quest for equality through brotherhood. As a result the four years between 1964 and 1968 were the most intense period of national division and civil unrest since the Civil War.[118]

Rather than an abundant harvest of equality resulting from racial harmony and brotherhood, the nation once again used the hammer of state as it embarked on a quest for equality of outcome. Equality of outcome would be sought through the efforts of thousands of politicians, judges, bureaucrats, and social engineers, each armed with a magnifying glass and carpenter's level.

But this new, disquieting definition of equality created another victim. In the march to a forced equality of condition or outcome, the higher goal of racial harmony and brotherhood had been trampled. As one can see from a half-century of legislative, judicial, and bureaucratic meddling, humanistic equality through leveling society is a fruitless, never-ending, and divisive task.

Racial harmony must be first priority in relations between the races. As racial harmony improves, gains in racial equality will occur over time. Without racial harmony, efforts to achieve racial equality are doomed. Thanks to the provocative and disingenuous Obama administration, racial harmony descended to its lowest level in a half century. Racial harmony can never be achieved by a government that attempts to micro-manage society through pronouncements, edicts, directives, laws, threats, and intimidation. Such attempts at moral suasion without a transcendent moral element are nothing more than governmental bullying.

Racial harmony will never be achieved by mobs, rioting, and the like. Long-term advancement in racial equality is one of the byproducts of racial harmony which must be rooted in the hearts of a majority of a society's citizens. Such racial harmony is made possible when the moral bearings of society are anchored in an understanding of right and wrong that flows from unchanging and eternal objective truths that do not originate with man.

True equality can only be achieved through brotherhood and right relationships. When the emphasis changes to racial equality as defined by humanism we see men compelled to descend to mediocrity and are stripped of position, possessions, brotherhood, and motivation to achievement.

―――

To understand which worldview best promotes the good society through a right relationship of man and his community, we began this chapter by examining human nature as impacted by the rival concepts of fraternity and equality. This examination leads us to recognize the importance of rootedness which rests on Weil's "...real, active, and natural participation in the life of a community, which preserves in living shape certain particular treasures of the past and certain particular expectations for the future." We must ask ourselves which worldview meets the human need of rootedness that implies connection and community. Put another way, from which does rootedness and sense of community arise—from the relational nature of fraternity or equality's emphasis of the individual and exaltation of self?

From the *Humanist Manifesto* we see that the central humanist value centers on the individual as opposed to relationship and more specifically fraternity. Secondly, we see humanistic egalitarianism as a disintegrating concept regarding human relationships (*brotherhood* and *fraternity*). The failures of humanism's egalitarian concepts in connecting man with his community are rooted in a false worldview which does not reflect human nature and the story of mankind.

In an attempt to mitigate the humanism's destructive effects on society through fragmentation and a loss of fraternity in its relentless pursuit of humanism's equality, three apostles have been recruited to support of humanism's goddess of equality: multiculturalism, tolerance, and diversity.

Multiculturalism – Christianity far exceeds humanism and other worldviews in its adaptation to and civil respect for diverse cultures and governments. From whence does this adaptation and respect come? First, Christianity offers truth and therefore provides the answers to life's basic questions which helps to bring order to one's soul and ultimately brings order to those societies in which Christians dwell. Truth provides a measure of *commonality* between men, a set standard by which men may interact with one another. Truth also engenders *trust* as it is exhibited in the lives of people that are followers of Christ *and* followers of His example. Second, Christianity does not have a political agenda other that adherence to principle. Therefore, it enters and resides quietly in various societies—from free to totalitarian. The essence of the humanists' concept of multiculturalism has its roots in the denial of absolutes, one of the cardinal doctrines of humanism, which translates into a moral relativism. Such a values-free approach, according to the humanists, makes it impossible to judge one period or era in relation to another or to say that one culture's ethic is superior to another. Therefore, we must agree that all belief systems are "…coexisting and equally valid."[119]

Humanists frequently point to multiculturalism as a source of cultural strength, but the reality is that cultures are strengthened by *differentiation*. The application of humanistic definitions of multiculturalism to a culture leads to fragmentation. The distinction between *differentiation* and multiculturalism is that *differentiation is "…only possible if there is a center toward which the parts look for their meaning and validation*" by which is meant the various parts look to the central cultural vision for their significance and justification. Under multiculturalism, the central cultural vision becomes subordinate to the various cultural entities whose parochial interests are deemed superior to that of the dominant cultural authority, that is, the central cultural vision. Therefore, multiculturalism tends to disunity and fragmentation among the various competing interests within the host culture.[120] Multiculturalism is merely a subset of the larger humanistic doctrine of cultural relativism as is tolerance, multiculturalism's corollary.

Tolerance – Christian teaching speaks unerringly in defense of the concept of universal human rights and why each person is obligated to respect the rights of others. The conflict with the humanist worldview regarding tolerance arises with the humanist belief that man is a social animal, and his morality results from his innate altruism, a moral instinct of selflessness, though not equally developed in all humans. For the humanist, the origin of man's morality evolved from his ability to connect value or benefit with behaving well toward others, but that value does not originate with the laws established by a supernatural God. The humanist solution to "chauvinistic ethnicity" and its consequent intolerance is to recognize a new inclusive ethnicity that certifies its membership in the world community. This inclusive ethnicity is to be achieved through: (1) recognition that the state must be secular in nature, (2) implementation of concepts and methodologies for achieving tolerance that transcend individual cultural boundaries, and (3) an adherence to humanist values beginning with recognition of humanistic definitions of universal human rights. Therefore, toleration begins with the denial of absolutes as no man or group can claim ownership of truth which is often the product of the free give and take of conflicting opinions. The humanist stance towards toleration is a reflection of moral relativism which is the antithesis of Christian belief and that of many other religions.

Diversity – The Christian's focus is not on individual differences but upon diversity's contribution to the whole of society, and from this emphasis comes unity. Unity is made possible when each member is recognized as an indispensable contributor to the body. This is not pursuit of the humanists' "greater good for humanity" as dictated by the state. Rather, it is *valuing the differentiation which supports the central cultural vision* derived from the collective worldviews of the culture. Humanism's diversity is a close kin of multiculturalism and focuses on the differences within society and not society as a whole. With emphasis on the differences, mass culture becomes nothing more than an escalating number of subcultures within an increasingly distressed political framework that attempts to satisfy the myriad demands of the individual subcultures. There is a loss of unity through fragmentation and ultimately a loss of a society's central cultural vision which leads to disintegration. Humanism's impulse for diversity is a derivative of relativism and humanism's perverted concept of equality.

If culture depends on unity and truth, the humanists' imposition of the leveling practices of multiculturalism, tolerance, and diversity in support of equality is an enemy of culture. As a result of the widespread acceptance of the humanists' perverted definitions, the central cultural vision of America has become blurred and is in danger of disintegration.

Contrary to humanism's weak substitute for fraternity, we see the truth of the biblical image of fraternity which is coherent, consistent, and gives orientation and direction for living life and therefore is reality. This reality becomes evident as we look at the images of God reflected in the permanent things of his creation that are universal to all of mankind for all periods of history and as revealed in the biblical record which gives clarity and detail to His plan for mankind.

Perhaps the best expression of God's view of equality between man and his community is found in the Apostle Paul's letter to the Galatians.

> But before faith came, we were kept under guard by the law, kept for the faith which would afterward be revealed. Therefore the law was our tutor *to bring us* to Christ, that we might be justified by faith. But after faith has come, we are no longer under a tutor. For you are all sons of God through faith in Christ Jesus. For as many of you as were baptized into Christ have put on Christ. There is neither Jew nor Greek, there is neither slave nor free, there is neither male nor female; for you are all one in Christ Jesus. And if you *are* Christ's, then you are Abraham's seed, and heirs according to the promise. [Galatians 3:23-29. NKJV]

Codes of behavior upon which cultures and societies must rest rely on *fraternity* and not equality. Fraternity and brotherhood resonate through history as they are the offspring of the seminal purposes of man—relationship with God and other men. The object of fraternity is other-directed and speaks of duty, congeniality, cooperation, and sense of belonging whereas humanism's egalitarian definition of equality focuses attention on self and results in egotism, alienation, division, and hostility.

Logic coupled with observation and experience leads us to accept the truth of the biblical worldview with regard to the importance and supremacy of fraternity in human relationships as opposed to the humanists' focus on the individual and their illusionary and disordering notions of equality.

10

Equality and Labor-Property Relationships

Many years ago before my mother passed away at age 79, we were talking about our life on the family dairy farm when my brothers and I were kids. For those that don't know, a dairy farm is a seven-day-a-week job with long hours, and as kids we thought everyone worked like that. Teasingly, I told my mother that if I knew then what I know now, I would have reported her and my father for child abuse! We both had a good laugh. While my brothers and I may not have appreciated it when we were children and teenagers, the instilled work ethic molded us, shaped our characters, and made possible many of the joys and blessings of life.

Before we describe the impact of the humanistic understanding of equality on labor and property, we must examine man's historical perceptions of each. We begin with the pagan and Christian worldviews regarding labor and property.

Labor

As our nation staggers toward the looming welfare state, work has become just another profane four-letter word. The denigration of work has been around for thousands of years and was very evident in the classical civilizations of Greece and Rome which viewed physical work as demeaning to all except slaves and the lower classes. In ancient Athens, one-third of freemen sat daily discussing the affairs of state in the court of Comitia while their slaves, who outnumbered citizens five-to-one, performed all manual labor. In the "bread and circuses," pleasure-seeking ancient Roman culture, it was again slaves who did all of the manual labor.[121]

But during the first century, at the eastern edge of the Mediterranean, a child was born that would give voice to God's view of the dignity of labor. His name was Jesus, the promised Messiah. His early disciples were mostly callus-handed fishermen, tradesmen, and even a local IRS agent. And the arch-persecutor-turned-apostle of this tiny Christian sect was a brilliant theologian and evangelist but also a tent-maker by trade. And the apostle Paul admonished the Thessalonian Christians that, "For even when we were with you, we commanded you this: If anyone will not work, neither shall he eat." [2 Thessalonians 3:10. NKJV] It was in the first century that Christians were driven from their homeland and made their first appearances in the Greco-Roman world. Because Christians believed in the dignity and honor of work, they were held with contempt by their Roman masters. Persecution arose, in part, because those strange Christian beliefs about work conflicted with the Romans' view of the world and also because of suspicions and jealousies of the Christians' prosperity due to their strong work ethic.[122]

But the first century Christian view of work was not a new philosophy but a reflection of the image of the Creator stamped on man, the pinnacle of His creation. Biblical instruction and admonitions regarding work are abundant. The first chapter of Genesis records God's labored in creating the universe. Not only does God work, He charged man with responsibilities and duties of being fruitful, replenishing and subduing the earth, and having dominion over all living creatures. When Adam and Eve were driven from the Garden of Eden because of their sin, God told Adam that "...Cursed *is* the ground for your sake; In toil you shall eat *of* it All the days of your life....In the sweat of your face you shall eat bread Till you return to the ground..." [Genesis 3:17b, 19a. NKJV] Notice that God did not impose work as a punishment for their sin. Rather, the curse was on the ground upon which they would toil. In other words, the curse was upon the conditions under which the work would be performed, not on work itself. But God loved man and would make possible a way for him to re-enter right relationship with God by sending His Son Jesus in human form as a babe. God chose to place his incarnate Son in a carpenter's home, and perhaps this gives us another insight into God's view of work.

With the decline and fall of the western half of the Roman Empire by the end of the fifth century, a remnant of the Christian heritage of the western portion of the Roman Empire was pushed northward into the sparse and hostile forests of France and western Germany. The inhabitants were Gauls whom the Romans had conquered and brought civilization at the beginning of the Christian era. To this group was added a smaller number of Teutonic invaders that had come from the east and hindered for a time the building of an organized social life and assimilation of the Mediterranean culture. Life was harsh in the pioneer wilds of northern Europe at the beginning of the Middle Ages around A.D. 500. However, out of this difficult and meager existence was built a cohesive and somewhat refined civilization, and the broad and general characteristics of their medieval society remained for centuries. Those characteristics and viewpoint, worldview if you will, became the ideas and ideals of Christendom which later became the foundations of the American experience from the earliest colonial days to the middle of the twentieth century.

Christendom's creedal reverence for work and its practical necessity amidst primitive conditions in the forests and clearings of early Europe produced the phenomenon of the middle class, non-existent before the advent of Christianity and now present in all of Western civilization. With the birth of the middle class came the reduction of poverty and its attendant diseases. And from the middle class arose political and economic freedom of a magnitude unknown in the history of the world to that time.[123]

Property

The end product of labor is property, be it a meager bowl of rice, a home, large farm, or factory. Labor and its twin private property are inextricably entwined and resist rationalist humanism's parsing. We have previously noted that the concept of justice requires that every man and woman in society are accorded the things that are rightfully their own, and this includes their private property. In an age of rampant egalitarianism, the one institution that stands against the rage to level all aspects of society is private property. Richard Weaver called it the last metaphysical right by which he meant that private property is one of the *absolute* rights of man. Christendom's creedal reverence for work produced private property and led to a middle class. Private property for the middle class was of such significant importance that the American Constitution defined the right to private property as indisputable.[124]

The right to private property surpasses the requirements and justifications imposed by the state. To have private property is perhaps an ultimate expression of privacy, or as Weaver called it, a "…sanctuary against pagan statism" in which rights are only valued or recognized if they support "…the purpose of the state and that, in turn, the utilitarian greatest material happiness for the greatest number."[125]

Two Views of Economic Order

One cannot understand the concept of equality and its impact on culture without an understanding of the competing means for organizing society. In Western civilization and much of the rest of the world, that competition is between capitalism and socialism. We shall briefly examine their origins and history, the worldview associated with each, and which does and does not contribute to the good society. Finally, we shall examine the heart of the conflict regarding equality that ultimately revolves around the status of private property and personal income under each system.

In the twentieth century, those holding the humanistic view of the world wrested the reins of power from leaders that believed that private property was an absolute right of man. In the humanist worldview man was basically good and equal at birth. Therefore, differences and inequalities were caused by the environment. Under humanist domination, the role of government was fundamentally changed to be one of eliminating inequalities in society. Consequently, humanistic prescriptions for righting the perceived wrongs of society were implemented and deemed superior to private property. These egalitarian prescriptions are the source of attack on private property. In the twentieth and twenty first centuries, the victor in the contest between socialism and capitalism will ultimately define the relationship of labor and private property with society.

The genesis of the conflict between capitalism and socialism arose from the large-scale industrialization in the Western world near the beginning of the nineteenth century. J. M. Roberts in his definitive *History of the World* stated that the magnitude of societal change produced by industrialization was the "most striking in European history since the barbarian invasions"…and perhaps the "…biggest change in human history since the coming of agriculture, iron, or the wheel."[126]

Capitalism, unlike socialism, was not invented and therefore is not a philosophy. Rather, capitalism is a long-term outgrowth of the natural workings of human motives and endeavors as they coalesced around the events of the late eighteenth and early nineteenth centuries. These events included great strides in agricultural production, increasing population, technological advances, replacement of human and animal labor with machines, increasing specialization, production in larger units, and centralization of the means of production. The engine that powered all of these aspects of human life and activity was capital which had been built up over centuries in places where a measure of societal stability led to investor confidence, and this confidence was found primarily in Western civilization.[127] Growth in agriculture and industrialization would have been impossible without capital investment. Yet, the relationship between commerce and capital was symbiotic. Capital grew when investments were successful, and successful investments unleashed demand for more capital.

But societal change of the magnitude and rapidity as described by Roberts was massively unsettling. The social fabric was stretched or torn as populations shifted from agrarian life to crowded cities, the development of new schools and change of educational requirements, and the emergence of new social classes as property and wealth were reshuffled to reflect new economic realities. Dislocation and human suffering were enormous during the initial stages of industrialization and devastating to whole generations. This suffering was seen in the bleak industrial cities, the exploitation of labor and especially children and women, and the loss of centuries of order, more specifically defined as a loss of place and purpose. The church reeled under attacks by the humanistic philosophies of the Enlightenment that offered other solutions to society's woes. Yet, the poverty of urban life of the times was perhaps no greater than that of the agrarian hovel except in the loss to the soul.

Efforts to recapture the soul would take much of a century and would never really be successful as deceptive definitions of man and his purpose would poison his consciousness by relegating him to animal status with no soul and therefore no need of God.

But the Church would not quietly cede Western civilization to the flood waters of industrialization and Enlightenment philosophies. Compassion was the Christian innovation in all of history and was evident in Christ's concern for the hurting and sick. From the earliest days of the industrial revolution, Christianity invaded the cities to not only save the soul but provide services and address societal ills for the hurting masses. Christian men of compassion fought to outlaw child labor in England, men such as William Wilberforce and Lord Shaftesbury. But Shaftesbury was the most determined and worked tirelessly for decades in Parliament to pass many bills that improved the lot of English children. The renowned preacher Charles Spurgeon said of Shaftesbury, "A man so firm in the Gospel of Jesus Christ, so intensely active in the cause of God and man, I have never known."[128] From such men and women came the likes of George Muller, a German who became a missionary to England in 1829. He established his first orphanage for girls in 1836, and by the time of his death in 1898, eight thousand children in numerous orphanages under his direction were being educated and cared for.[129] Other organizations were birthed such as the Salvation Army (founded in London in 1865 by William and Catherine Booth) that ultimately provided worldwide relief for millions of the poor and destitute. Although General Booth died in 1912, his and his wife's work would continue and expand into over one hundred countries by the end of the twentieth century.[130] These are just few of the thousands that immersed themselves in the grit and poverty of the eighteenth century to address vast societal changes and deprivations caused by industrialization.

But taking its cue from enlightenment rationalism, there was another voice offering different solutions. Unlike Christianity, it was not interested in saving the soul but redefining man and society. The rise of socialists and socialism generally corresponded with the emergence of the industrial age near the beginning of the nineteenth century.

> Both words were first commonly used in France around 1830 to describe theories and men opposed to society run on market principles and to an economy operated on laissez-faire lines, of which the main beneficiaries (they thought) were the wealthy. Economic and social egalitarianism is fundamental to the socialist idea…All socialists, too, could agree that there was nothing sacred about property, whose rights buttressed injustice; some sought its complete abolition and were called communists. "Property is theft" was one very successful slogan.[131]

At this point we must more specifically describe capitalism and socialism. *Capitalism* is an "...economic system characterized by private or corporation ownership of capital goods, by investments that are determined by private decision rather than by state control, and by prices, production, and the distribution of goods that are determined mainly by the operation of a free market." *Socialism* is "...any of various economic and political theories advocating collective or governmental ownership and administration by the means of production and distribution of goods..." [132] Interestingly, the first American dictionary published by Noah Webster in 1828 did not have a definition for either socialism or capitalism as these were rather new concepts in the emerging industrial age.[133]

In the very earliest years of Europeans on the American continent, socialistic answers were sought to replace the Christian work ethic as the North Star for organizing society. Because of their isolation from the civilized world, Jamestown and the Plymouth Colony stand as great laboratory experiments regarding questions as to the validity and worthiness of socialistic principles. In the isolated and controlled environment of the New World, communism of an almost pure variety, failed miserably in its initial years as laziness and inefficiency trumped thrift and industry. As the colonists abandoned their experiment in socialism, the colonies flourished.

Karl Marx's ideas regarding socialism presented in *The Communist Manifesto* became the twentieth century's grand socialist experiment which led to the enslavement of a third of humanity behind the iron and bamboo curtains. For three quarters of a century, the consequences of these socialistic systems were poverty, misery, and death unparalleled in the history of mankind. Socialism still holds sway over much of Eastern civilization.

But our collective memory is short and socialism's propaganda machine is strong. As a result Christianity and its values are being rapidly abandoned in Western societies in favor of a humanistic worldview requiring socialistic solutions to address society's problems. As a result, socialism is destroying the middle class and its indispensable Christian work ethic, and many in America are being seduced by the allure of a bread and circuses culture.

The displacement of the work ethic by the actions of the American government's social engineers since the 1960s has had a multitude of far-reaching consequences. Just one example is the humanistic welfare solutions that have fractured the concept of family by substituting governmental assistance to unwed pregnant teenage girls. Fathers are not required to work and provide for the mother and child for whom they are responsible. This welfare system perpetuates itself through ensuing generations that repeat the cycle. The direct consequences of the institutionalization of illegitimate births in American life have dramatically raised the illegitimacy rate (6% in 1963 to 41% in 2014) with consequent increases in rate of drug abuse, dropout rate, crime rate, and incarceration rate.[134] And those percentages have continued to climb in the years since 2014.

In the mid-1990s Congressional welfare reforms required those seeking welfare to work. However, this requirement was removed by an executive order of President Obama in 2012. Additionally, governmental subsidies provided by the Affordable Care Act were subsequently determined to be a *disincentive to work* by those receiving subsidies with a consequent loss of 2.5 million jobs over the next three years according to a Congressional Budget Office Report.[135]

The operation of man's fallen human nature exposes the soft and rotten underbelly of the tenets of socialism and humanism's faith in mankind and their co-commitment to the principle of the greatest-happiness-for-the-greatest-number which humanists consider to be the highest moral obligation for humanity as a whole. The operation of human nature conflicts with man-made socialistic solutions to the problems of life, and the end result is failure. People fail, families fail, and cultures ultimately fail. The socialists' false view of man's nature leads to poverty, starvation, and loss of freedom. The antidote is a rejection of socialism and a return to the Christian work ethic.

That capitalism has once again been resurrected as the bad boy that creates a broken society and robs the poor should be no surprise to any student of the history of the nineteenth and twentieth centuries. Capitalism's nemesis is socialism. The opposing concepts for organizing society have found different homes in the two dominant worldviews in Western civilization—Christianity and humanism. Both capitalism and socialism claim the badge of freedom, but their definitions of freedom are substantially different. Generally, socialism speaks of a "freedom from..." while capitalism espouses a "freedom to..." This simple distinction makes a great difference in how we live our lives. Whichever worldview prevails will dominate and organize society and determine how we, our children, and our grandchildren will live our lives. This battle lies at the heart of the culture wars and currently revolves around cries for income equality.

Capitalism is synonymous with free enterprise and free markets while socialism is associated with planned economies and state control. As previously noted, the out-workings of these concepts revolve around the definition of freedom to which both claim allegiance. Socialism cannot be separated from its parent and patron—humanism. Humanism requires socialism as socialism is the chain-mail glove into which the hand of humanism fits and uses to enforce its vision of societal order. Written ten years before this book, the following is a quote from the author's book *Ye shall be as gods-Humanism and Christianity-The Battle for Supremacy in the American Cultural Vision* which describes the loss of freedom under socialism.

> The humanist definition of freedom presumes to loose man from the bondage of mores, norms, tradition, and distant voices of the past. However, the humanists' definition of freedom, which co-joins the maximization of individual autonomy with the humanist-created primacy of the greatest good for the greatest number, is a false freedom. A society organized around the tenets of humanism cannot remain free as it will be pushed to one end or the other of the anarchy-totalitarian continuum of government. In reality, such humanistic concepts of freedom coerce the individual through the requirement of a *general commonality of thought and action* which is *forced downward from the state to the individual*. However, the central cultural vision of any society must command unity for it to exist and prosper in ordered harmony. Such unity must filter up from individuals, not be coerced or forced down on society. Without such unity filtering up from individuals, there can be no order to the soul or society, and without such order society deteriorates over time and eventually disintegrates.[136]

By contrast, although there is an affinity between capitalism and Christianity, Christianity does not require capitalism nor does capitalism require Christianity. The affinity lies in freedom defined as lack of coercion. A free market (capitalism) "…is not 'Christian in and by itself; it is merely to say that capitalism is a material by-product of the Mosaic law.' In other words, capitalism is a *by-product of Christianity's value of freedom applied to economic life and activities*."[137] [emphasis added]

That Christianity values freedom should be no surprise. God valued freedom so much that he gave freewill to man, the pinnacle of His creation. God wishes to share his love and eternity with His creation, but He does not coerce or compel man in the spiritual realm nor does he wish man to be coerced in the economic realm on this earth as does fascism, socialism, and communism.[138]

Capitalism is most successful when it is the most moral. It is not coincidence that the greatest freedom and economic prosperity occur in countries where Christianity is and continues to be the dominant worldview. Capitalism that arose during the period of industrialization was often wild and reckless as a new-born colt that thrashes about until it steadies itself. It was the moral suasion of Christianity that helped steady capitalism and correct its excesses.[139]

How is it then that socialism has a growing following around the world and even in wildly successful capitalistic countries such as the United States? Writing seventy years ago amidst humanity caught up in a conflagration of death and destruction during World War II, F. A. Hayek gave insight into the answer.

> The most effective way of making people accept the validity of the values they are to serve is to persuade them that they are really the same as those which they, or at least the best among them, have always held, but which were not properly understood or recognized before...And the most efficient technique to this end is to use the old words but change their meaning...Few traits of totalitarian regimes...are characteristic of the whole intellectual climate as the complete perversion of language, the change of meaning of the words by which the ideals of the new regimes are expressed. The worst sufferer in this respect is, of course, the word "liberty" (freedom).[140]

The trashing of capitalism began in earnest by the mid-nineteenth century when Karl Marx, atheist and communist, wrote *Das Kapital* (Capital) in which he saw labor as both distinct from and an antithesis to capitalism. Thus began collectivist's propaganda efforts at replacing capitalism's definition as being free markets and free enterprise to that of being a merciless evil preying on the proletariat.[141]

In answer to capitalism's critics, the late Pope John Paul II framed the issue well in 1996 when he asked whether the failed communist states in Eastern Europe should opt for capitalism. In reply to his own rhetorical question he stated,

> If by 'capitalism' is meant an economic system which recognizes the fundamental and positive role of business, the market, private property and the resulting responsibility for the means of production, as well as free human creativity in the economic sector, then the answer is certainly in the affirmative.[142]

However, less than two decades later, Pope Francis would dignify leftist denigration of capitalism in his 224-page *Evangelii Gadium*, or Joy of the Gospel, that attacked capitalism as a form of tyranny and called on church and political leaders to address the needs of the poor.[143]

> 53. ...Today everything comes under the laws of *competition and the survival of the fittest*, where the powerful feed upon the powerless. As a consequence, masses of people find themselves excluded and marginalized: without work, without possibilities, without any means of escape. [emphasis added]
>
> 54. In this context, some people continue to defend trickle-down theories which assume that economic growth, encouraged by a free market, will inevitably succeed in bringing about greater justice and inclusiveness in the world. This opinion, which has never been confirmed by the facts, expresses a *crude and naïve trust in the goodness of those wielding economic power* and in the sacralized workings of the prevailing economic system... [emphasis added]
>
> 56. While the earnings of a minority are growing exponentially, so too is the gap separating the majority from the prosperity enjoyed by those happy few. This imbalance is the result of ideologies which defend the absolute autonomy of the marketplace and financial speculation. Consequently, *they reject the right of states, charged with vigilance for the common good, to exercise any form of control...*[144] [emphasis added]

One must ask which man has experienced socialistic totalitarian societies and therefore has a better insight into the horrors of socialism as compared to the worthiness of capitalism. Certainly it is the Polish Pope John Paul II whose leadership along with that of Ronald Reagan and Margaret Thatcher resulted in the downfall of communism in much of the world and the liberation of millions.

Pope John Paul II's intransigence against socialism was evident from the beginning of his papal reign when he disciplined Latin American liberationist priests within the church who had incorporated a Marxist orientation as one of the pillars of liberation theology. In the late 1960s a rebellious sociology had dramatically developed in Latin America. This sociology regarded the underdevelopment of the continent as a consequence of the capitalist market system. As a result, undeveloped countries were exhorted to reject the capitalist market system in favor of a socialist economy. As this new sociology was absorbed, liberation theology emerged from its wake. But John Paul's message to the Latin American Catholic church was that Marxism cannot be regarded as an instrument of sociological analysis, being a wrong vision of the human person and a biased scientific method. Rather, liberation theology must be centered on Christ the Redeemer.[145] In the most recent years of his papacy, Pope Francis has unequivocally endorsed, promoted, and adhered to liberation theology and its Marxist worldview. His beliefs have been influenced by and are a product of the highly socialistic orientation of liberation theologies prevalent in South America. Pope Francis's socialistic orientation becomes abundantly evident when reading *Evangelii Gadium*.

We have examined capitalism and socialism's definitions and the battle of words and worldviews surrounding the adversaries. Now we shall look at the heart of the conflict that ultimately revolves around the status of private property and personal income.

The imposition of income equality inevitably leads to loss of property rights and loss of freedom. Therefore, to understand the demands for income equality, we first must contrast the status of private property in socialistic and capitalistic societies. Communists consider private property as theft. Specifically, Marx' and Engels' Communist Manifesto written in 1848 states: "The theory of Communists may be summed up in the single sentence: The abolition of private property."[146] The opposing views of property and private income are well illustrated by the words of several Founders.

> The moment the idea is admitted into society that property is not as scared as the laws of God, and there is not a force of law and public justice to protect it, anarchy and tyranny commence. Property must be secured or liberty cannot exist.[147] [John Adams]

> Government is instituted to protect property of every sort...[It] is not a just government where the property which a man has in his personal safety and personal liberty is violated by arbitrary seizures of one class of citizens for the service of the rest.[148] [James Madison]

> The man who truly understands the political economy best...will be least likely to resort to oppressive expedients, or to sacrifice any particular class of citizens to the procurement of revenue. It might be demonstrated that the most productive system of finance will always be the least burdensome.[149] [Alexander Hamilton]

Three-quarters of a century later, President Abraham Lincoln confirmed the beliefs of the Founders when he spoke to the New York Workingmen's Democratic Republican Association regarding property, wealth, and the wealthy.

> Property is the fruit of labor. Property is desirable, is a positive good in the world. That some should be rich shows that others may become rich, and hence is just encouragement to industry and enterprise. Let not him who is houseless pull down the house of another; but let him labor diligently and build one for himself, thus by example assuring that his own shall be safe from violence…I take it that it is best for all to leave each man free to acquire property as fast as he can. Some will get wealthy. I don't believe in a law to prevent a man from getting rich; it would do more harm than good.[150]

How is it that the socialistic quest for income equality has risen to new heights of power and respectability in American society given the opposing beliefs of the Founders and most Americans to the mid-twentieth century? The answer has its roots in a new interpretation of the general welfare provision of the Constitution's Article I, Section 8, which states that, "The Congress shall have Power To lay and collect Taxes, Duties, Imports and Excises, to pay the Debts and provide for the common Defense and general Welfare of the United States…" Some at the time of its writing interpreted this clause as granting to Congress broad powers that exceeded those powers specifically enumerated in the Constitution. But James Madison, one of the Constitution's drafters and regarded as the father of the Constitution, did not agree with the more liberal interpretation and claimed that such a reading was inconsistent with the concept of limited government. Additionally, imputing broad powers to the general welfare provision renders the enumerated powers redundant.[151] However, the Supreme Court in 1936 dramatically distorted the interpretation of the clause that was held for 150 years. Unleashed by the new meaning, Congress was permitted to distribute "…federal bounties as a demonstration of 'concern' for the poor and needy."[152]

It was relatively easy for liberals in and out of government to portray their "concern" for the poor and needy as a matter of justice. The pursuit of the humanistic definition of justice began in the 1970s with American academics that broke with previous political philosophers from the ancient Greeks to the American Founding fathers with regard to the purpose of the state. The academics now argue that the fundamental task of the state is to end inequality which rests on the core belief that inequality is intrinsically bad and even intolerable and that government should do something about it.[153]

This Enlightenment concept of human equality flows from the humanistic assumption of the perfectibility of man. Under this concept, what men are comes from experience. Therefore, men are equal at birth, and differences and inequalities arise due to environment. The goal of humanists is to achieve an egalitarian society (and thus eliminate inequalities due to environment) through political means in which man, achieving perfect equality in their political rights, would at the same time be perfectly equalized and assimilated in their possessions, their opinions, and their passions. When humanists failed to achieve equality of outcome through political equality, the levelers demanded economic democracy, a new and expanded humanist definition of equality. However, economic democracy still means an equality of condition as opposed to equality of opportunity and is to be achieved through recognition of invented or synthetic rights coupled with broad but non-specific egalitarian ideals. However, as society is leveled with guarantees of certain outcomes to its citizens, political equality suffers.

In order for government to accomplish its newly defined purpose of eliminating all inequality, it is necessary to impose a socialistic system. Therefore, capitalism had to go, and the typical means to trash capitalism is to portray capitalism as unjust, unfair, lacking concern for the poor, greedy, and dishonest. Think of the Occupy Wall Street protests of recent times. The essence of their protests and arguments was that justice is not possible under a capitalistic system…and the state must do something about it. Under assault from government, academia, and other spheres of American life, many in America consider "capitalism" to be a dirty word. But the majority of those that hold this view have little memory of the negative effects of alternative approaches used to organize society. And the vast majority of American universities which are filled with professors who embrace the humanistic worldview (and its inherent socialism) and have little interest in presenting historical truth. Rather, for humanists and others of the Enlightenment crowd, their paradise will ultimately be achieved as humanity moves ever upward and onward in its continual quest for perfection through the disappearance of the individual soul into universal equality.

The humanistic meaning of this pervasive equality is clearly stated in *Humanist Manifesto II's* eleventh common principal, "The principle of moral equality must be furthered…This means equality of opportunity…" But, the meaning of "equal opportunity" is immediately and drastically corrupted to mean an equality of outcome by humanist requirements. To further clarify the intent of the signors of the *Manifesto*, the document states that, "If unable, society should provide means to satisfy their basic economic, health, and cultural needs, including whatever resources make possible, a minimum guaranteed annual income."[154]

Income inequality is the bogey-man used by the liberals to advance the socialist agenda and destroy capitalism. Emotions are aroused by appeals to class consciousness, envy, and hatred that damages cultural unity and pushes the nation along the road to disintegration. They have been successful because of the American citizenry's ignorance of the nation's founding principles, decades of deconstruction of Constitutional safeguards by liberal judges, and the domination of the institutions and leadership of American life by those holding a humanistic worldview,

The founding Americans relied on order that rested upon a respect for prescriptive rights and customs as opposed to the egalitarian notions of French philosophers during the French Revolution. This difference was made clear by John Adams' definition of equality which strikes at the heart of what it really means—a moral and political equality only—by which is meant equality before God and before the law. This definition does not teach that all men are born to equal powers, mental abilities, influence in society, property, and other advantages. Rather, all men are born to equal rights before God and the law and by implication equal opportunity.[155]

We have stated that a good society is marked by a high degree of order, justice, and freedom. In the name of equality, the imposition of humanistic leveling concepts do great harm through an imposition of a socialistic ordering of society which leads to injustice and loss of freedom with respect to labor and private property.

11

Equality – Traditional v. Progressive Education

One must understand the difference between education and instruction. Instruction is the imparting of facts and principles with regard to a body of knowledge. Education is much more comprehensive and includes not only instruction but the shaping of the mind and personality, that is, one's worldview as how one understands and lives life. In the modern world the elementary and secondary schools and the universities control the process of educating children and young adults. Those possessing that control significantly influence the worldviews of their pupils. Therefore, the individuals and institutions that control the education process have great influence upon whether a society's central cultural vision is preserved or destroyed.[156]

Individual worldviews of a society's inhabitants may be as varied as fingerprints in which no two are alike. But through tradition and experience a society achieves a general symmetry of thought, understanding, and action regarding the world, how it works, and how one ought to live. This communal understanding leads a society to a unified central cultural vision. Put another way, a culture's central vision is a synthesis of the collective worldviews of its citizens. But that central cultural vision is not merely a passive recipient but also acts as a center of authority which serves to reinforce, protect, and preserve that central vision with a subtle and pervasive pressure to conform which may range from cultural peer pressure to moral and legal restraints.

By its very nature, a culture must discriminate against that which is alien and which over time, if left unchecked, would destroy its central cultural vision to which it believes to be true, worthwhile, and worthy of defending. A central cultural vision must unify and therefore is of necessity exclusionary and inward-looking. The culture that becomes all-inclusive loses its focus and will decline, disintegrate, and be replaced by a central cultural vision which is alien to its citizens' worldviews and values.

Apart from being a unifying force for culture, a society's central cultural vision must be based on one other essential component to insure the survival of its central cultural vision—ultimately, it must be based on truth. The collective worldviews we have chosen to call a central cultural vision must achieve a structure, design, or pattern by which a semblance of societal order is achieved. Here we must define truth as immutable, absolute, or eternal. If a central cultural vision fails to align itself with truth, then that society fails to give orientation and direction for living life because of a lack of *coherence and consistency* within the individual and collective worldviews. At the beginning of this book, it was stated that if a person's actions and beliefs are not internally coherent and consistent, the conflict must be resolved or over a period of time that person's integrity and mental health will be diminished. Likewise, a loss of coherence and consistency within the central vision of a culture leads to a loss of trust, allegiance, and unity of its citizens which are necessary for survival of the culture. Therefore, the requirement of coherence and consistency points to the undeniable importance of truth in a society's central cultural vision.

Germany in the early twentieth century is but one modern example of a society based on an inherently false view of the world. In education, science, scholarship, and music, no nation of the world had attained more than Imperial Germany. Furthermore, it was internally perhaps the most law-abiding of all nations. However, the post-WWII world remained puzzled at Germany's "collective derangement" (that is, a false and dysfunctional central cultural vision) given its veneer of education, rationality, and scientific and cultural progress. J. N. Roberts described this collective derangement.

> In many ways, Germany had been one of the most progressive countries in Europe; the embodiment of much that was best in its civilization. That Germany should fall prey to *collective derangement* on this scale suggested that *something had been wrong at the root of that civilization itself.* The crimes of the Nazis had been carried out not in a fit of barbaric intoxication with conquest, but in a systematic, scientific controlled, bureaucratic (though often inefficient) way, about which there was little that was irrational except the appalling end which it sought.[157] [emphasis added]

German society had many of the elements necessary to preserve its central cultural vision. It was unified, exclusionary, and inward-looking. Yet, there was something wrong at the root of its civilization which no amount of education and scientific advancement could cure. Humanistic, scientific, rational men failed to see the truth that an indelible stain marked the soul of mankind. Rejection of God and pretenses of ethnic superiority could not erase this stain which is the root of evil that is found within the soul of every human being that ever lived. Christians call it *original sin*. In spite of sitting at the pinnacle of scientific and rational civilization, German society was doomed because its central cultural vision rested on a false view of mankind.

We have briefly examined the different meanings of education and instruction, worldview and its importance in society, and the elements necessary to sustain a central cultural vision (without which it is destined for failure). With this foundation, we are ready to address the ascendance of *progressive education* in America which has undermined America's central cultural vision upon which the nation was founded and prospered.

Education in America to the twentieth century

Time and the passing of generations are on the side of those promoting humanistic concepts of equality because it is possible for the educators of our children to disconnect them from their history and cultural roots of their ancestors. That is precisely what has happened over the last 120 years in the American classrooms.

The worldview and values of the American colonists up to and including the founding of the nation were undeniably Christian in origin and practice. Sherwood Eddy wrote that it was "…religion, and often religion at its best as in the case of the persecuted Pilgrims of Plymouth, [that] was to become a dominating factor in the founding of the new world of America." And, of the new nation that arose one-hundred fifty years later he wrote, "No country on earth was ever founded on deeper religious foundations. This was America's priceless heritage." [158]

Both at the time of the European settlement of North America and at the founding of a nation, the cultural and moral values of the colonists and America's Founders were rooted in the biblical Christianity. With regard to education of their children, these early Americans embraced the biblical worldview in which parents were admonished to "Train up a child in the way he should go, And when he is old he will not depart from it." [Proverbs 22:6. NKJV] The implication is plain that the *primary* purpose of a child's training was transmission of cultural and moral values. This was the unshakable view of Samuel Adams, known as the "Father of the American Revolution," and who instigated the Boston Tea Party, signed the Declaration of Independence, and served in both the Continental Congress and the U.S. Congress. His views on education paralleled those of many other Founding Fathers.[159]

> Let divines and philosophers, statesmen and patriots, unite their endeavors to renovate the age, by impressing the minds of men with the importance of educating their little boys and girls, of inculcating in the minds of youth the fear and love of the Deity…in short of leading them to the study and practice of exalted virtues of the Christian System.[160]

Next to the Bible, the principle textbooks used by colonists and citizens of America to the beginning of the twentieth century were *The New England Primer* and *McGuffey's Reader*. *The New England Primer* first published about 1690 was the only elementary textbook in America for a half century, retained its central role in primary education until 1800, and continued as a principal beginning textbook throughout the 19th century. The eighty-page Puritan primer contained lessons in the alphabet, spelling, short religious instruction, commands to piety and faith, and Bible questions.[161]

Between 1836 and 1920, 120 million copies of the *McGuffey's Reader* textbooks were sold. The *Readers* hailed American exceptionalism, manifest destiny, and America as God's country although in more secularized terms beginning with the 1879 version. In a 1927 *Saturday Evening Post* article titled "That Guy McGuffey," Hugh Fullerton wrote that, "For seventy-five years his (McGuffey's) system and his books guided the minds of four-fifths of the school children of the nation in their taste for literature, in their morality, in their social development and next to the Bible in their religion."[162]

The churches were the principal founders of the first colleges and universities in the American colonies and whose purpose was for the training of pastors. During the eighteenth and nineteenth centuries, colleges and universities expanded their academic portfolios, and the cultural ties between the Church and higher education gradually weakened. However, the weakening ties generated little cultural controversy because the explicitly Christian and generally conservative ends of education were understood by the great majority of Americans. Nevertheless, as the end of the nineteenth century approached, "…the breach separating the universities and the churches widened suddenly and culminated in the extraordinarily rapid and dramatic 'disestablishment' of conservative Protestantism from North American academic life from about 1890 to 1930."[163]

The heir to conservative Protestantism as the authority in education was called the "progressive" theory of education. From the early years of the twentieth century to the present day, the progressive theory of education has swept through all levels of education from pre-schools to the universities. The theory of progressive education is a derivative of humanism. The egalitarian concept of equality is an important component of the theory of progressive education. Before we examine this theory of education, we must first understand how it displaced conservative Protestantism as the cultural authority in education.

With rare and disastrous exceptions such as communism's substantial separation of children from parents, the formation of the worldviews of children was the province of their parents since the beginning of man's time on earth. From primitive peoples huddled around communal campfires in the millennia of the past to the generations of the early twentieth century, children received their worldview and its related values from their parents and extended family, and the local church and community almost universally reflected those same values and worldview. Children in colonial America and the post revolution United States attended local schools whose teachers and textbooks strongly reflected their parents' values. As parents shape the worldview of their children, their beliefs and the values reflected by the central cultural vision are preserved and strengthened.

Progressive education – Origins and inter-workings

We shall now dissect the origins and inter-workings of the progressive philosophy in education. It is only in modern times that the point of view (worldview) of the educator has been allowed to conflict with the point of view of the culture and its citizens (central cultural vision). This began happening in America at the beginning of the twentieth century. Education progressives began to systematically undermine three hundred years of established American cultural traditions and beliefs. Richard Weaver called this "...a virtual educational *coup d'état* carried out by a specially inclined minority. This minority has been in essence a cabal, with objectives radically different from those of the state which employed them." Writing just before his death in 1963, Weaver believed that there were hopeful signs that the progressivism of education was drawing to a close.[164] But Weaver's hope was misplaced for he failed to see the insidious nature of humanism not only infected education but was creeping into and would capture much of the leadership of all institutions of American life by the end of the century. The education establishment and the state have become willing accomplices, inseparably joined in transforming American culture into a sterile, *equalitarian* landscape whose humanistic arbiters dictate the cultural values and understandings of right and wrong to be imposed on the masses.

Without doubt the father of progressive education was John Dewey. Dewey's admirers called him the greatest American philosopher and the philosopher of American democracy. His views and teachings during his exceptionally long career would influence many facets of American life—art, knowledge, education, morals, politics, science, and religion—and publication of his writings spanned seventy years from his first philosophical essay in 1882 to his death. The breadth of change during Dewey's lifetime is astounding. Dewey was a grocer's son born in Burlington, Vermont, on October 20, 1859, while James Buchanan was president, a year and a half before Abraham Lincoln's inauguration. With remembrances of the Civil War, he would live to see two world wars and the atomic age by the time of his death in 1952, just five years before Sputnik would herald the beginning of the space age.[165]

Following two years teaching high school in Pennsylvania, Dewey entered graduate work at John Hopkins University in 1882. He received his PhD in 1884 and began teaching courses in ethics, history of philosophy, logic, and psychology at the University of Michigan. With the exception of one year spent at the University of Minnesota, he would stay at Michigan until moving to the University of Chicago in 1893 as the head professor in philosophy. Dewey made his final move in 1905 to the Department of Philosophy and Psychology at Columbia University in New York City from whence he would retire in 1930. During those years he was associated with the University's Teachers' College, and shortly after his arrival at the University he would be "recognized as the leader of the 'progressive movement' in education." Following retirement, he would remain at Columbia as Professor Emeritus in Residence.[166]

Psychology, published by Dewey in 1896, was the first American textbook on the "revised" subject of education. It became the most widely read, quoted, and used textbook in American schools of education. Beginning with his twenty-five-year affiliation with Columbia University's Teachers' College, Dewey's "…writings shaped the 20th Century U.S. curriculum…"[167] His ideas on education would extensively permeate American education, and the devastating results are still being felt today.

One measure of John Dewey's impact on American education can be judged by the level of criticism that was provoked by his teachings. In March 1959, President Eisenhower severely condemned Dewey's philosophy: "Educators, parents, and students must be continuously stirred up by the defects in our education system. They must be induced to abandon the educational path that, rather blindly, they have been following as a result of John Dewey's teachings."[168] For an individual deceased for seven years to have his work and philosophy receive the stinging rebuke of a sitting president, that individual's influence on American life, for good or ill, must be viewed as substantial.

What is the essence of this philosophy that engendered so much controversy? Dewey's progressive educational agenda was framed by child-centeredness and psychology.

> In the enlightenment tradition…Progressives saw human nature as essentially good or neutral, rejecting the view of original sin…The child, in this view, develops naturally through reason and experience. Child-centeredness thus locates the source of authority in the self and human nature, rather than in God and the Supernatural. Because human nature is good and because the child is innately programmed to develop

naturally, education must nurture the intrinsic development and expression of child nature rather than break it or submit it to authority. This conception lies at the basis of modern primary education.[169]

Sidney Hook was an ardent defender of Dewey and identified three essential elements of his philosophy of progressive education. First, Dewey emphasized that all education is fundamentally a result of *experience*.[170] Children were taught that an understanding of morality flowed from reason based on experience and that there was *no one morality good for all societies*. Reason through science became the determinant of what was good for society and replaced character education as modeled by Judeo-Christian morality. In other words, the standards of the new morality are dictated by science and reason.[171] In Dewey's philosophy, there is no absolute, no transcendent being, no room for supernatural religion, and nothing beyond the possibilities of concrete human experience. Value and meaning in life exist in humanity and flow from individual and collective self-realization through civilization.[172]

The second of the essential elements of the philosophy of progressive education is *democracy*. But Dewey knew that democracy could function poorly. Dewey's was a *moral* democracy "…committed to an equality of concern for each individual in the community to develop himself as a person." For Dewey, this education equality meant that common quantitative standards were inapplicable in the educational process.[173] Put another way, Dewey's educational democracy is a *moral equality* that disconnects intellectual and emotional growth from traditional, recognized, and time-honored measures. Rather, individual achievement and growth must be measured against those distinctive elements that are intrinsic and important to the individual. Hook calls Dewey's moral equality or ideal democracy "…the most revolutionary principle in the world because its scope embraces all social institutions."[174]

The third essential of progressive education is the *emphasis on the scientific method* in education coupled with rejection of a supposed anti-scientific dogmatism. According to Hook, the scientific method was the supreme authority in judgment of fact and value. "Every alternative involves at some point an institutional authority which, historical evidence shows, lends itself to abuse, which claims itself to be above all interests and becomes the expression of a particular interest invested with the symbols of public authority."[175] As a result, Dewey embraced scientific psychological study as the means to train humans as opposed to the tenets of religion that embraces the supernatural. Dewey felt that religion based on the supernatural was destructive because it "…attributes human achievement and purpose to man in isolation from the world of physical nature and his fellows." In other words, religions based on the supernatural are divisive in that, by their very nature, men are set apart from the world. Likewise, Dewey rejected God because such a being is outside of nature. The ideal existence occurs when that existence "...has its roots in natural conditions."[176]

In summary, under Dewey's progressive education model, children are disconnected from the eternal and time-honored truths, standards of morality, and traditions passed down from generations of our ancestors in favor of a supposedly pragmatic reliance on experience and one's feelings. Educational success is gauged by the measure of a child's happiness, how he feels about himself, and his focus on what is important to him. Discipline, mastery of a body of knowledge, and an understanding of eternal truths and values are subjugated to concerns of self-esteem and self-actualization. Lastly, through a corrupt and prejudiced use of the scientific method, progressive education adherents saturate their students with the humanistic worldview that rejects the supernatural, religion, and God in favor of naturalism or materialism (aka humanism). It is important to notice the content and structure of each of these essentials of progressive education have a distinct leveling effect among students which is essential in achieving a pervasive egalitarianism in society.

Richard Weaver succinctly and superbly describes the disastrous consequences of progressive education's revolt against the traditional idea of education.

> Knowledge, which has been the traditional reason for instituting schools, does *not* exist in any absolute or binding sense. The mind, which has always been regarded as the distinguishing possession of the human race, is now viewed as a tyrant which has been denying the rights of the body as a whole. It is to be "democratized" or reduced to an equality with the rest. Discipline, that great shaper of mind and body, is to be discarded because it carries elements of fear and compulsion. The student is to be prepared *not* to save his soul, or to inherit the wisdom and usages of past civilizations, or even to get ahead in life, but to become a member of a utopia resting on a *false view of both nature and man*.[177] [emphasis added]

Hook was correct when he called progressive education's concept of *moral equality or an ideal democracy* "...the most revolutionary principle in the world because *its scope embraces all social institutions*."[178] Of the three essentials of progressive education, it is progressive education's doctrine of educational equality that has seeped most deeply into the heart of every American social institution. This has occurred because four generations of Americans have been subtly indoctrinated by the progressive education system with the humanist concept of moral equality which was quite foreign to the American understanding of equality during the three hundred years of life on the continent since the arrival of the first Europeans during the first two decades of the 1600s to the first part of the twentieth century.

Moral equality, as defined and envisioned by humanists and their progressive education minions, *rests upon a false and utopian worldview* that violates the purpose of education, undermines the supremacy of parental influence on their children's beliefs, teaches a false understanding of the nature of man, rejects the limitations of science and reason in defining morality, and denies the ultimate source of morality and truth. Because of saturation of the tenets of progressive education in American schools and universities and it's push for moral equality, many if not most Americans in the twenty first century have become ultra-self-absorbed, academically ignorant, devoid of concepts of right and wrong, possessed of a victim mentality, undisciplined, disrespectful of the law, and consumed with "rights" as opposed to obligations to family, community, nation, and God.

For almost one hundred years, a major conflict has grown between values and beliefs of the formerly dominant American central cultural vision and the values and beliefs of the ascendant progressive theory of education and its proponents. In this conflict, America's Godly heritage has been systematically removed or suppressed by a radical clique of educators and their allies in a largely successful campaign to undermine and change American society's traditions and beliefs and thereby radically alter the nation's central cultural vision. Of all American institutions under assault, the subversion of American culture through the humanistic educational establishment's progressive movement represents the greatest single threat to the central cultural vision upon which the nation was founded. It is severing the roots of American order which is leading to injustice and loss of freedom.

Part III – The Goddess of Equality and the Destruction of the Good Society

Over the course of its history America has been a stunning success as a result of the creation of the good society. The reasons for this success are that the colonists and Founders recognized and understood that a well-ordered, just, and free society was created when the pattern or order of that society reflected the nature and character of God.

As noted at the beginning of this book, the virtues of order, justice, and freedom form the trinity necessary to achieve a good society. To better understand the status and qualities of order, justice, and freedom which make them necessary for a good society, we look at the deeper meaning of virtue. Principally, the nature of virtue can be summed up as conformity to a standard of right, morality, and a particular moral excellence.[179] Order, justice, and freedom are virtues because they infuse and are held together by those things we call human universals, first principles, eternal truths, and norms. These virtues serve as guides to our reasoning and instruct us on the way life works and how one must act. A good or virtuous society is achieved when the concepts of order, justice, and freedom are rightly understood and applied and therefore point to truth, right action, and morality, all of which are required to create and sustain a good society. From this platform of virtues we have examined the modern expansive definition of equality (i.e., egalitarianism) presented by humanism as opposed to mankind's much narrower understanding of equality through the millennia.

The degree to which a society is good or bad depends on its adherence to the virtuous principles of order, justice, and freedom, of which order has primacy. An attack on one of endangers the others and threatens that society. Where order, justice, and freedom are under attack and the good society fails to defend its moral and social order, then it will sink into disorder, injustice, and bondage and eventually disintegrate.

The defense of the good society must center on a restoration of a high moral and civil order that encourages and supports true justice and freedom. To defend and elevate the general moral and civil order is to defend the various institutions of American life. Humanistic forces are invading every facet of American institutions and life: the church, government, politics, economics, education, the sciences (physical and human), media, entertainment, popular culture, and American life in general. But order is of the first magnitude, and the prerequisite for the defense of the moral and civil order begins with a defense of the language and freedom of speech.

12

Assault on Language and Free Speech

Egalitarianism's assault on language – Attacking Truth and Promoting the Lie

Richard Weaver believed "…that a divine element is present in language. The feeling that to have power of language is to have control over things is deeply imbedded in the human mind." Throughout the ages language has been the means of achieving order in culture. Knowledge of truth comes through the word which provides solidity in the "shifting world of appearances."[180]

However, for the humanist-liberal-progressivist, the shifting world of appearances is more important and useful than objective truth which they deem to be a fiction. When truth is unhooked from the anchor of objective meaning, it ceases to be truth and becomes either mere perception or consensus of opinion, shackled to time, and cannot be objective or eternal.

Paul Greenberg wrote about the larger issue of the decline of the American language at the hands of modern political operatives.

> They know that the way to win an election is to muffle unpleasant truths and soften hard principles. Besides, clarity is hard work. It's so much easier to fuzz the message and so write around any inconvenient facts that may disrupt the smooth flow of currently fashionable patter.[181]

In modern American debate dominated by the humanistic worldview, talking points have supplanted truth and sound-bites are substituted for deep thinking. Words have gained power to obscure truth and history through the machinations of humanist redefinition. Modern demagogues dressed as humanistic politicians, pundits, and intellectuals who obscure both truth and history have borrowed a page from V. I. Lenin, founder of the Communist party and leader of the Russian Revolution.

> We must be ready to employ trickery, deceit, law-breaking, withholding and concealing truth. We can and must write in the language which sows among the masses hate, revulsion, scorn, and the like, toward those who disagree with us.[182]

This is the technique or protocol of the humanist-liberal-progressivist: *Deny* the existence of objective, eternal truth; *redefine* key concepts such as truth, freedom, justice, and equality; and *ignore* or *revise* history to promote the belief that America was created as a secular nation and thereby drive the Christian worldview from the public square. Because of what the humanists, liberals, and progressivists have sown throughout the culture, Americans who disagree with them are targets of hate, revulsion, scorn, and violence. Thus, we have identified differing views as to the meaning of truth as the origin of the vast chasm separating the humanist and Christian combatants in the war for supremacy in the central cultural vision of America.

Weaver called words the storehouse of our memory.[183] In our modern age humanists have effectively used semantics to neuter words of their meaning in historical and symbolic contexts, that is, words now mean what men want them to mean. By removing the fixities of language (which undermines an understanding of truth), language loses its ability to define and compel. As the meaning of words is divorced from truth, relativism gains supremacy, and a culture tends to disintegration without an understanding of eternal truths upon which to orient its self. The end result is that the people of the Western world have lost the memory of what words mean and therefore who they are, from whence they came, and where they ought to be going.

Egalitarianism's assault on free speech

Humanism's egalitarian lever used to shift society requires socialism as the means for organizing society in order to achieve equality. Socialism demands an *elastic* language. For humanists, truth is defined in terms of cultural relativism which requires a suspension of judgment since all belief systems contain some truth within while no one belief system has all the truth. Therefore, all social constructions are culturally relative as they are shaped by class, gender, and ethnicity. Thus, there can be no universal truths because all viewpoints, lifestyles, and beliefs are equally valid. As a result, no man or group can claim to be infallible with regard to truth and virtue. Rather, truth is a continually shifting array of dissimilar claims and opinions which mean that truth can be manufactured to fit the agenda.

In 1949, George Orwell wrote *1984*, which provides a glimpse of the reality of life under socialism. This grim novel is about an omnipresent government set in Airstrip One, formerly Great Britain but now merely a province of Oceania, a super-state ruled by a political system called English Socialism. Oceania's leaders are the Inner Party, a privileged elite headed by Big Brother, the pseudo-divine party leader who uses mass media, propaganda, and a cult-like following to create his idealized, heroic, and god-like public image. Oceania is a land of constant war, omnipresent government surveillance, and public mind control. However, the oppressive nature of the regime is justified by Big Brother and the Party in the name of the supposed greater good.[184] At the beginning of the third decade of the twenty-first century, the Communist Chinese Party is a modern incarnation of Orwell's Oceania. Ironically, the Chinese communist government came to power in 1949, the same year as Orwell's book was published.

Big Brother's and the Party's control of the public's mind is achieved with the assistance of the *Ministry of Truth* which is responsible for propaganda and revisionism of history and controls the news media, entertainment, the arts, and publishing. The *Ministry* falsifies the historical record where necessary to conform it to the government-approved version of events. To assist in its propaganda and revisionist efforts, the government invented *Newspeak*, a language used to limit freedom of thought and other expressions of individualism and independent thinking which are considered thought crimes.[185] The major social media empires controlled by China in the East and billionaire humanists in the West are the modern purveyors of *Newspeak*.

Words are the means by which order is achieved in society. The dominant worldview of the members of a society determines the elasticity allowed in defining the meaning of words within the language and ultimately the meaning of truth and the freedom of the individual. The winner of the war between the worldviews contending for dominance in Western civilization will determine the fate of mankind. The Judeo-Christian worldview leads to truth and freedom. Humanism leads to relativism and socialism whose ultimate end is totalitarianism.

A modern prophet from the mid-twentieth century foresaw the effects of an elastic language with regard to the meaning of words. In his 1944 book, *Road to Serfdom*, F. A. Hayek (1899-1992) has much to say about the language of socialism which he considers synonymous with totalitarianism. Whether it is the socialism of extensive redistribution of incomes through taxation and the institutions of the welfare state or socialism through the nationalization of the means of production and central planning, Hayek rightly believed the outcome is essentially the same for both systems—totalitarianism.[186] And it is socialism's perversion of the language (words and their meaning) that is of particular concern. Once the sources of all information are under the control of a totalitarian regime, it has the power to mold the minds of the people. The minds of the people will then be indoctrinated with the precepts of the regime and no others will be tolerated. The moral consequences of totalitarian propaganda are destructive to one of the essential foundation of all morals, that is, "...the sense of and respect for truth."[187] Hayek described the means whereby language is perverted by socialism's propaganda.

> The most effective way of making people accept the validity of the values they are to serve is to persuade them that they are really the same as those which they, or at least the best among them, have always held, but which were not properly understood or recognized before…And the most efficient technique to that end is to use the old words but change their meaning. Few traits of totalitarian regimes are at the same time so confusing to the superficial observer and yet so characteristic of the whole intellectual climate as the complete perversion of language, the change of meaning of the words by which the ideals of the new regimes are expressed. The worst sufferer in this respect is, of course, the word "liberty." It is a world used as freely in totalitarian states as elsewhere.[188]

The quest for equality in a socialistic society becomes an officially enforced equality. Enforced equality is labeled the new freedom or "collective freedom" which is not the freedom of the individual "…but the unlimited freedom of the planner to do with society what he pleases."[189]

In the Judeo-Christian worldview, truth is the foundation of all civil and moral societies, and the meaning of truth is obscured in direct proportion to the elasticity allowed in defining the meaning of words within a language. For 1500 years the source of truth for much of Western civilization has been the Bible. The meaning of words such as truth, freedom, good and evil were relatively *inelastic* within the Christian worldview. Their meanings were based on absolutes called by various names: permanent things, universals, first principles, eternal truths, and norms. These absolutes were revealed to man by God through His creation and His revelation to the ancient Hebrews and first century Christians.

The defense of language and speech in the good society

The prophecies of Orwell, Hayek, and Weaver were published in their respective books between 1944 and 1950. The fulfillment of their prophecies with regard to the perversion of the meaning of words and the suppression of free speech is abundantly evident in twenty-first century America.

The ascending humanistic worldview requires that society be organized upon socialistic principles. During the last half of the twentieth century, the redefinition of the meanings of certain words has become the feedstock of socialism's propaganda machine: multiculturalism, diversity, freedom, tolerance, good, evil, right, wrong, justice, freedom, and equality to name just a few. The new meanings are being used to mold the thinking of society in support of a humanistic worldview and its socialistic agenda. To this we add the suppression of free speech.

The acid that eats at the integrity of truth and morality is relativism. Relativism is the child of the false and destructive worldview of humanism that is tied to time and therefore temporal. Humanism and other false religions may ascend and dominate for a season, but the seeds of destruction lie in their own falseness. Truth is eternal and therefore a permanent binder that transcends time. Truth rests in the unadulterated word. "In the beginning was the Word, and the Word was with God, and the Word was God...And the Word became flesh and dwelt among us... For the law was given through Moses, *but* grace and truth came through Jesus Christ." [John 1:1, 14a, 17. NKJV] In response to Pontius Pilate's question regarding Jesus' kingship, Jesus answered, "You say *rightly* that I am a king. For this cause I was born, and for this cause I have come into the world, that I should bear witness to the truth. Everyone who is of the truth hears My voice." [John 18:37. NKJV] Truth is reality, and it is the nature of man to seek and know truth. To know God is to know truth.

What must Americans to do in defense of the language and free speech in the good society? For the answer we look to the words of three giants of the twentieth century who defended the good society: Aleksandr Solzhenitsyn, Dietrich Bonhoeffer, and Martin Niemöller.

Aleksandr Solzhenitsyn

Solzhenitsyn (1918-2008) was born in Russia and studied mathematics, philosophy, literature, and history at the university level. He was a thrice decorated for personal heroism as a Russian Army Officer during the fight against the Nazis in World War II. In 1945 he was arrested for criticizing Stalin in private correspondence and sentenced to an eight-year term in a labor camp. From that experience he wrote *One Day in the Life of Ivan Denisovich* which was published in 1962, the first of many books. In 1970 he was awarded the Nobel Prize for Literature. In 1974, he was stripped of his citizenship and expelled from the Soviet Union whereupon he moved to Vermont with his wife and four sons.[190]

Solzhenitsyn's background, experiences, and powerful words in defense of truth speaks far louder than the din of lies shouted by egalitarianism's *Ministry of Truth* and its toadies including spineless politicians, the corrupt media, universities in name only, complicit megacorporation billionaires, ranting Hollywood leftists, self-proclaimed "intellectuals," and many corrupt voices/false teachers in the Church. Such lies cannot long stand against timeless truth of which God is the author and finisher.

Solzhenitsyn gives both the diagnosis of the plight of the good society and a prescription for preserving its Judeo-Christian cultural heritage and its attendant freedom.

> In keeping silent about evil, in burying it so deep within us that no sign of it appears on the surface, we are implanting it, and it (evil) will rise up a thousand fold in the future. When we neither punish nor reproach evildoers . . . we are ripping the foundations of justice from beneath new generations.
>
> The simple step of a courageous individual is not to take part in the lie. One word of truth outweighs the world.[191]

The defenders of the good society must raise their voices in the defense of the language and free speech from the lies and distortions of radical egalitarians. Silence only emboldens the evil doers and digs the graves of our children and grandchildren's moral and civil order, justice, and freedom.

Martin Niemöller and Dietrich Bonhoeffer

At the beginning of 1933, the German church stood at a crossroads. The great majority of German Lutheran churches chose the path of Hitler and the Nazis instead of the teachings of Jesus Christ.[192] There was a minority of Christians and churches in Germany that opposed Hitler and the apostatized German Christians. The resistance centered within the new "Confessing Church" led by Dietrich Bonhoeffer, Martin Niemöller, and a few others. As Nazi pressure was ratcheted up against the dissenting churchmen, Bonhoeffer and Niemöller were criticized by their fellow churchmen for opposing Hitler and his policies. Eventually over two thousand would choose the route of appeasement and safety and abandoned support of Bonhoeffer and Niemöller's efforts in resisting the Nazis. "They believed that appeasement was the best strategy; they thought that if they remained silent they could live with Hitler's intrusion into church affairs and his political policies."[193]

In the late summer of 1933, Niemöller wrote a letter to a friend about his opposition to Hitler.

> Although I am working with all my might for the church opposition, it is perfectly clear to me that this opposition is only a very temporary transition to an opposition of a very different kind, and that very few of those engaged in this preliminary skirmish will be part of the next

struggle. And I believe that the whole of Christendom should pray with us that it will be a "resistance unto death," and that the people will be found to suffer it.[194]

In early 1934 from the pulpit of his church in the Berlin suburb of Dahlem, Niemöller spoke of the coming trials that faced the German church.

> We have all of us—the whole Church and the whole community—we've been thrown into the Tempter's sieve, and he is shaking and the wind is blowing, and it must now become manifest whether we are wheat or chaff! Verily, a time of sifting has come upon us, and even the most indolent and peaceful person among us must see that the calm of a meditative Christianity is at an end…
>
> It is now springtime for the hopeful and expectant Christian Church—it is testing time, and God is giving Satan a free hand, so he may shake us up and so that it may be seen what manner of men we are!...
>
> Satan swings his sieve and Christianity is thrown hither and thither; and he who is not ready to suffer, he who called himself a Christian only because he thereby hoped to gain something good for his race and his nations is blown away like chaff by the wind of time.[195]

In 1937, Niemöller and more than eight hundred other churchmen were arrested and imprisoned for their opposition to the Nazis. Following release from prison after eight months, Niemöller was immediately arrested again as a "personal prisoner" of the Führer himself and spent the next seven years in Dachau, one the Nazis' most infamous concentration camps. He was freed by the Allies in 1945.[196] After the war, in his sorrow for not recognizing and speaking out in the early days of the Nazi rise to power, Niemöller penned this sorrowful message.

> First they came for the Socialists, and I did not speak out—Because I was not a Socialist.
>
> Then they came for the Trade Unionists, and I did not speak out—Because I was not a Trade Unionist.
>
> Then they came for the Jews, and I did not speak out—Because I was not a Jew.

Then they came for me—and there was no one left to speak for me.[197]

Dietrich Bonhoeffer was discussed in chapter 8 with regard to his views on church-state relationships. Bonhoeffer knew well the cost of silence in the church when faced with evil in the public square. His ardent faith and boldness in confronting evil cost him his life. He called silence when faced with evil what it was…sin.

> We have been silent witness of evil deeds; we have been drenched by many storms; we have learnt the arts of equivocation and pretense; experience has made us suspicious of others and kept us from being truthful and open…Will our inward power of resistance be strong enough, and our honesty with ourselves remorseless enough, for us to find our way back to simplicity and straightforwardness?[198]

> Silence in the face of evil is itself evil, God will not hold us guiltless. Not to speak is to speak. Not to act is to act.[199]

The words of Solzhenitsyn, Niemöller, and Bonhoeffer all carry the same message. Defenders of the good society *must not remain silent*. We must speak out with truth and take action to confront the evil of humanism and its handmaidens—egalitarianism's lies and falsehoods and socialism's corrupt order.

In our world of progressive education, scientism, and mass media, the semanticists have captured the linguistic high ground through redefinition of key concepts. Regarding the consequences thereof, Weaver cut to the heart of the matter.

> Just as soon as men begin to point out that the word is one entity and the object it represents is another, there set in a temptation to do one thing with the word and another different thing with the object it is supposed to represent; and here begins that relativism which by now is visibly affecting those institutions which depend for their very existence upon our ability to use language as a permanent binder.[200]

However, in the end, cultures and their component institutions do not survive which rest on the false dialectical pronouncements, definitions, and dogma of humanism. On the contrary, the long-term survival and prospering of a culture depends on its apprehension and incorporation of those things we have called eternal and unchanging truths or universals.

13

Erosion of the Principles of American Civil Order

Birth of the civil order of the good society

It all began as a tiny ship approached the shores of a primitive continent called America. Historian Paul Johnson in his massive *A History of the American People* called the arrival on December 11, 1620 of an old wine ship at New Plymouth "...the single most important formative event in early American history." The *Mayflower* contained a mixture of thirty-five English Calvinist Christians including some who had lived in exile in Holland to escape religious persecution in England. All were going to America for religious freedom. They were Separatist Puritans who had despaired of reforming the Church of England and its episcopal form of government and heavy influence of Catholic teaching. They were accompanied by sixty-six non-Puritans who had other motives for going to the New World. The two groups contained forty-one families.[201]

The Pilgrims, as these separatist Puritans would become known, weren't the first colonists to arrive. In 1607 the first English colony was established at Jamestown by gentlemen-adventurers, indentured servants, and landless men attempting to better themselves. The best men of the Jamestown colony brought with them English traditions of fair-mindedness, freedom, reverence for the common law, and a sense of government that looked to the common interest and general needs of society. But the Puritans of Plymouth were completely different as to personality and motivation. Johnson described their various members as "...the zealots, the idealists, the utopians, the saints...immensely energetic, persistent, and courageous...creative too but ideological and cerebral, prickly and unbending, fiercely unyielding on occasions."[202]

Paul Johnson's belief in the singular importance of the Pilgrims' arrival as the formative event in early American history rests on the monumental influence of the Pilgrims in shaping future generations of Americans. The Pilgrims established the model for faith, family, community, and governance which was followed to a large degree by Americans over the next two hundred years. They came not as individuals but as a community and not primarily for earthly gain but to create God's kingdom on earth. This sense of community was formalized in a remarkable document signed barely three weeks before their arrival. Having endured two months of a winter voyage in the turbulent North Atlantic amid the discomforts of a tiny and crowded ship, forty-one heads of households gathered in the main cabin of the ship and signed the

Mayflower Compact which pledged them to unity and the provision of a future government.[203]

> In the Name of God, Amen...Having undertaken *for the Glory of God, and Advancement of the Christian Faith*, and the Honour of our King and Country...Do by these Presents, solemnly and mutually in the Presence of God and one another, covenant and combine ourselves together into a civil Body Politick, for our better Ordering and Preservation, and Furtherance of the Ends aforesaid; And by Virtue hereof do enact, constitute, and frame, such just and equal Laws, Ordinances, Acts, Constitutions, and Offices, from time to time, as shall be thought most meet and convenient for the general Good of the Colony; unto which we promise all due Submission and Obedience.[204] [emphasis added]

Here we see that the Mayflower Compact represented far more than just a commercial venture based on a secular civil arrangement to secure unity and a form of governance for the moment. The Pilgrims had solemnly and mutually pledged in the presence of God and each other to a "civil Body politick" under "just and equal laws...[for the] furtherance of the glory of God." This simple document foreshadowed a theme that reverberated throughout the colonies over the next 150 years and led to the American Revolution. It put forth the idea that a just and equal society must rest on the foundation of religious faith. It recognized that government flowed from the governed—under God. It also recognized that there was a close connection between government and religious faith.[205] But for a time the colonists struggled to discover how the church-state relationship was to be properly constituted and limited according to the tenets of the Bible. Although fitfully at times throughout America during the colonial period, the proper constitution of that church-state relationship would occur 167 years after the Pilgrims' arrival on the shores of America.

Civil Order codified by the American Constitution

The government of any social organization must create some form of civil order—either good or bad. If America is the good society to which we desire to defend, then we must look to the American Constitution to determine what type of civil order (form of government) the Founders created. The American form of government was established by the Constitution of 1787 and the Amendments thereto. The brief statement of the kind of civil order sought by the Founders is found in the six purposes described in the preamble to the seven articles of the Constitution:

> We the people of the United States, in Order to form a more perfect Union, establish Justice, insure Domestic Tranquility, prove for the common defense, promote the general welfare, and secure the Blessings of Liberty to ourselves and our Posterity, do ordain and establish this Constitution for the United States of America.[206]

The primacy of freedom of religion and the free exercise thereof, freedom of speech, freedom of the press, the right of people to peaceably assemble, and to petition government is found in the First Amendment. The Second Amendment imposes on government the duty of security of a free State including the right of the people to keep and bear arms. Amendments Three, Four, and Five protect its citizens' person and personal property from government excess and over-reach.

From the Preamble and the first five Amendments, we see in the civil order established by the founders the great value placed on justice and freedom for the citizenry. These are the standards woven into the civil order, coupled with the moral order of the Judeo-Christian worldview. From these three (moral and civic order, justice, and freedom), the good society was established and flourished.

Erosion of American Civil Order

But this civil order has suffered considerable erosion over the last 150 years. In America and the remainder of Western civilization, the social organization of civil government has progressively moved toward secularization, pluralization, and privatization.

In a secularized culture, religion, its fundamental beliefs, the source of those beliefs, and the institutions that promote those beliefs and ideas are little valued and no longer viewed as socially significant in directing the affairs of men and women in that culture.[207]

In a pluralistic society that has been secularized there exist a number of worldviews contending for allegiance of its citizens. But no single worldview is allowed to dominate other than the anti-religious secular-humanistic worldview (its central cultural vision) which regards all sectarian (religious) worldviews as having equal worth or value but which have no voice in a secular society.[208]

Privatization is "defined as the socially required and legally enforced separation of our private lives and our public personas; in effect, privatization mandates that issues of ultimate meaning be relegated to our private spheres."[209]

Essentially, secularization states that the Christian church has no significant role in directing culture and defining its moral imperatives. Pluralization has demeaned the value of Christian truth and its message by equating it with all other competing worldviews and their false versions of truth. And finally, privatization socially and legally purges Christianity's voice from the public square.

The maintenance, preservation, and direction of the good society cannot be effectively charted without fixed reference points which are the universals, norms, eternal truths, permanent things, and ancient voices of the past. The relativistic cultural ideas and trends of a humanistic society and their leaders bent on progress without a supernatural God have been caught up in the swirl and noise of the moment and thus have forsaken those fixed reference points. The outworking and consequences of the deviations from the course laid down by the good society are often unrecognizable to a humanistic culture and its leaders until it is too late to adjust the rudder of the ship of state as it steams forward, oblivious to the looming shoals of anguish, pain, despair, destruction, and death that lay ahead.

Where should society look to find those invaluable reference points? The words of the poet Samuel Taylor Coleridge give us a clue. "If men could learn from history, what lessons it might teach us! But passion and party blind our eyes, and the light which experience gives is a lantern on the stern which shines only on the waves behind us."[210] Coleridge's point is that we must look to history for guidance to the future, but our backward look requires more than a cursory, fragmented glance at the recent past. History must be studied and pondered to catch the whole sweep of truths it can teach. But the ascending humanist worldview wants nothing to do with the dead carcass of history and its delusions of a supernatural God.

Humanism through its egalitarian concept of equality is the poison that is eating away at the inner workings of the good society. It is the toxin that is destroying order, justice, and freedom. As a result, the good society in America is suffering a sickness in its soul.

Sickness in the soul of the American Republic[211]

The soul of a republic can be viewed as its central cultural vision—that collective worldview that animates and informs all of society and over-arches both the civic order and moral order. Rooted in their hearts and minds, that vision is also supported and invigorated by its citizens. However, the American Republic is comparable to the demise of high civilizations in ancient times in that certain elements of alienation have entered into America's central cultural vision which has weakened its citizens' love for and belief in its compelling purposes.[212] These elements deny the value and truth of the Republic's beleaguered central cultural vision and attempt to replace it with multiple centers of cultural vision based on arbitrary and ever-changing inventions of man. In other words, the sickness of the American Republic's soul is cause by a *loss of unity* and the *denigration of the truth* upon which the nation was founded.

Loss of Unity

To understand what is meant by loss of unity, we must briefly review a concept presented in chapter 3. Unity is made possible when is it presupposes a general commonality of thought and action. A culture is formed and begins ordering its world to bring the satisfactions for which it was created. Order requires a general unity of a society and can only be achieved and order maintained through the imposition of directions upon its members. These directions, limits, and required behaviors radiate through a center of authority with a subtle and pervasive pressure to conform. This pressure may range from cultural peer pressure to moral and legal restraints. Those that do not conform are repelled of necessity. Thus, in any culture there are patterns of inclusion and exclusion. Without such patterns, cultural unity is lost, and the culture becomes unprotected and disintegrates over time. The intrinsic nature of culture compels that it be exclusive rather than all inclusive. Cultures fail and disintegrate without the power to reject that which is alien and does not adhere to its central force—its central cultural vision.[213]

In America, disunity is pandemic in every facet of cultural life including government, education, family, politics, standards of moral behavior, the arts, economics and business, and religion. Disunity is also evident as the war of words flow from the Internet, newspaper and magazine headlines, and TV and radio sound bites. This disunity occurs because of the ubiquitous attack on America's original central cultural vision.

Denigration of Truth about God and man

For a culture to survive over the long-term, its central cultural vision must be based on truth. Put another way, a culture's central cultural vision must be informed by and reflect that which is true. In Western civilization, the Christian worldview reflects this truth. Since the nation's founding, this central cultural vision has been under assault by the humanistic worldview that gained ascendance in Europe during the eighteenth century. The core of the battle revolves around the truth about the nature of man—who he is.

In the Christian worldview, the Supreme Being (God) created matter out of nothing and formed the universe. He impressed certain principles upon that matter, from which it can never depart, and without which it would cease to be. These principles dictate rules of action and applies to animate and inanimate objects. These "laws of nature" must invariably be followed by the universe and the created matter therein. One exception was man, the pinnacle of God's creation, who was allowed to choose to follow or depart from those principles as they relate to human nature. Those principles are truths that are intrinsic, timeless, and are essential elements that provide a coherent and rational way to live in the world. As we have stated numerous times, these absolutes are called by various names: permanent things, universals, first principles, eternal truths, and norms. These absolutes were revealed to man by God through His creation and His revelation to the ancient Hebrews and first century Christians.

It is important to once again summarize the disordering concepts of the humanistic worldview that are used to disparage the truth about God and man. This denigration is centered on cultural relativism which requires a suspension of judgment since all belief systems contain some truth within while no one belief system has all truth. For humanists, all social constructions are culturally relative as they are shaped by class, gender, and ethnicity. Therefore, there can be no universal truths because all viewpoints, lifestyles, and beliefs are equally valid. As a result, no man or group can claim to be infallible with regard to truth and virtue. Rather, truth is relative, situational, and continually evolves over time. Man is merely the end-product of a long evolutionary process that occurred by chance and not the result of some supernatural Creator.

The central cultural vision of colonial Americans and the nation's Founders was built on the truth of Christian principles. The assault by the opposing forces of humanism was repelled until the early twentieth century when they began gaining critical mass in the various spheres of American life.

Tampering with Justice

Societies dominated by humanism impose political concepts that create a different principle of ordering society that is contrary to universal truths. Those concepts are often born of ignorance and may be initially popular, but dissatisfactions invariably arise because those societies have tampered with the "nature of things."[214]

One of the victims of this tampering is justice. The concept of justice is a universal truth, a thing of permanence that transcends the whole of man's time on this planet and pertains to all cultures. Since man is presumed not corruptible man, the levelers of society bend justice to arbitrarily and capriciously impose the latest standards dictated by the passions of the moment. Prescriptions of fairness, impartiality, and right action derived from an authority above the state and built up over the centuries are consigned to the dumpster of history because they are antiquated or the product of superstition and ignorance. In summary, the unchanging definition of justice over the millennia has been changed to fit the humanists' worldview. But no amount of humanist tampering will change the heart of man with regard to a right understanding of fairness, impartiality, and right action required in a civil society.

Loss of Freedom

Benjamin Franklin succinctly described the linkage of freedom with the good society when he said, "Only a virtuous people are capable of freedom. As nations become corrupt and vicious, they have *more need of masters.*"[215] [emphasis added] Freedom requires a civil order entrusted to a virtuous people. Loss of the good society results in corrupt and vicious society which means more rulers, more laws, and less freedom. John Adams agreed with Franklin's assessment.

> We have no government armed with power capable of contending with human passions unbridled by morality and religion. Avarice, ambition, revenge, or gallantry, would break the strongest cords of our Constitution as a whale goes through a net. Our constitution was made only for a moral and religious people. It is wholly inadequate to the government of any other.[216]

In essence, true freedom requires a virtuous civic order linked with a virtuous moral order, the sturdy heart of the good society.

Daily we are seeing the loss of freedom in America. As citizens turn from a Christian worldview, they are unable to orient and guide themselves internally with regard to ethical and moral issues. But this is the picture of life in 21st century America as we see the power and reach of the humanistic state and its freedom-killing legions of masters rapidly extending their reach and control over all spheres of the civil order.

Christianity and Christian principles that once permeated and bonded with the principles of civil government formed the basis for America's exceptionalism. But in the 21st century exceptionalism is in great danger of becoming merely tedious mediocrity wrapped in the shroud of boredom if not bondage. If America rejects Christianity and Christian principles as the underpinnings of its moral and civil order which inform and guide American civil government and culture, America will cease to be great and will no longer be exceptional. As a consequence its citizens will lose their freedoms.

14

The Spiraling Decline of American Moral Order

As has been expressed numerous times throughout this book, the good society rests upon and is a product of moral order and civil order which are derived from their alignment with objective truth. In this chapter we turn our attention to the decline of moral order which deals with the soul of man as opposed to civic order by which is meant how the body politic organizes and governs itself. All societies have may have a degree of moral and civil order but which are defective to the degree that one or more of its essential components (order, justice, and freedom) are not aligned with objective truth.

We begin with the attack on the moral order of the Founders which rests upon the Judeo-Christian understanding of God and His nature, the creator of the universe and all therein. Like civic order, moral order is rooted in the cultural universals, norms, eternal truths, and permanent things as revealed by His creation and the biblical revelation. It is this moral order which Satan attempts to destroy.

Moral goodness – the stuff of moral order in the good society

We gain an interesting insight into how moral goodness (and by default, moral order) was perceived during the revolutionary period and in the first years after the founding of the American Republic. In Noah Webster's 1828 *American Dictionary of the English Language,* the third definition of virtue is:

> *Virtue* - Moral goodness; the practice of moral duties and the abstaining from vice, or a conformity of life and conversation to the moral law. In this sense, *virtue* may be, and in many instances must be, distinguished from *religion*. The practice of moral duties merely from motives of convenience, or from compulsion, or from regard to reputation, is *virtue*, as distinct from *religion*. The practice of moral duties from sincere love to God and his laws, is virtue and religion. In this sense it is true…Virtue (without religion) is nothing but voluntary obedience to truth.[217] [emphasis in original]

Moral order requires moral goodness. Virtue, in and of itself, is commendable but when joined to the sincere love of God it becomes moral goodness (true virtue) and such is the stuff of the moral order of the good society. Put another way, the good society is made possible by moral goodness co-joined with the Christian religion's eternal truths, universals, and permanent things revealed by God in His creation and the biblical revelation, i.e., moral order.

Moral order of the good society led astray – the lure of humanism's equality

We trace the rise of the seductress of equality in man's history to the first chapter of Genesis.

> And the serpent said unto the woman, Ye shall not surely die: For God doth know that in the day ye eat thereof, then your eyes shall be opened, and *ye shall be as gods*, knowing good and evil. Genesis 3:4-5 KJV. [emphasis added]

This was man's ultimate quest for equality, to be equal with God and so has it been to the present day. Man's quest for equality with God did not end when he was cast out of the garden. It remains a favorite tool of the Tempter and has been evident in every facet of man's history on the planet. In his massive commentary on the Bible written near the beginning of the 1700s, Matthew Henry wrote of the Tower of Babel. In Genesis 9 God told Noah and his sons to be fruitful and multiply and fill the earth. In chapter 11 we find that they had indeed become fruitful and multiplied but the various tribes had not spread out as Noah and his sons had agreed because the people did not want to disburse and instead chose to build a city on the plain of Shinar.[218]

> And they said, "Come, let us build ourselves a city, and a tower whose top *is* in the heavens; let us make a name for ourselves, lest we be scattered abroad over the face of the whole earth." [Genesis 11:4. NKJV]

Henry's commentary points to three reasons for the people's actions. First, the tower whose top might reach to heaven spoke of a defiance of God, or at least an attempt to rival him. Second, they wanted to make a name for themselves. The tower was to be a lasting symbol of their pride and ambition. Third, the tower was built to prevent their dispersion. Here Henry points to the vaulting ambition of Nimrod who hoped to establish a universal monarchy over which he would exercise power but do so under the pretense of achieving a common safety.[219] God confused their language and as a consequence they were forced to separate and spread across the earth.

Here we see that the spirit of the humanism which is the spirit of the world planted by Satan in the heart of man while in the Garden. This humanistic spirit rooted in the original sin of mankind survived the Great Flood and was scattered over the face of the whole earth.

The quest for equality and the rise of humanism

The Greeks gave form and body to the humanistic spirit in which "*man is the measure*" was a mere echo of the serpent's words, "*Ye shall be as gods*." Almost two millennia after the Greeks' enthronement of "man the measure," the late Renaissance and Enlightenment birthed *modern humanism* that fundamentally challenged man's thinking and view of the world. Man would not only be God's equal, he would dethrone Him and take his place. God was to be banished to the dustbin of history as an anomaly in the evolutionary chain of human progress, a fairytale spun in a distant, dark, and ignorant past.

As we have seen throughout this book, the humanistic definition of equality since the eighteenth century has been the lever that attempts to dislodge the Judeo-Christian worldview dominant in Western civilization for 1500 years and in America since the arrival of the first colonists in the early 1600s. The imposition of humanism's equality into the realm of *social, political, and economic rights and privileges* and its focus on the removal of any and all inequalities among humankind has changed the meaning of the universals of order, justice, and freedom.

Humanism's modern concepts of the moral order no longer portray truth, morality, and right action as flowing from God's laws. Therefore, we see the humanistic worldview must be inherently defective (including that of egalitarianism's equality). One need only look at the destruction, human misery, and death to understand the disastrous effects that flowed from communism and fascism during the twentieth century as a result of loss of the Judeo-Christian moral order. In American society, the quest for humanism's moral order beginning in the last half of the twentieth century has clearly devastated much of the good society as defined and implemented by the founders and maintained by the citizenry for 150 years after the nation's founding.

Humanists continue to successfully peddle their egalitarian lies in spite of the evidence that the Judeo-Christian worldview reflects ultimate truth or reality in every sphere of life makes possible the good society. The goal of achieving a good society by following the virtues of order, justice, and freedom that flow the universals, norms, and divine truths *must be subservient* to the humanists' egalitarianism. Put another way, the good society must be sacrificed upon humanist altars to pay homage to the goddess of equality.

How can this be? Why is the humanists' delusional exaltation of self and its attendant need for forced equality so compelling that it blinds them to objective truth, especially in light of man's miserable history during his time on the earth? The answer is given by the Apostle Paul as he instructed the Thessalonians about events that would begin to occur with the establishment of the Church in the first century. Those events will dramatically increase as the end of the last days approaches just before the second coming of Christ.

> Let no one deceive you by any means; for *that Day will not come* unless the falling away comes first, and the man of sin is revealed, the son of perdition... For the mystery of lawlessness is already at work; only He who now restrains *will do so* until He is taken out of the way. And then the lawless one will be revealed, whom the Lord will consume with the breath of His mouth and destroy with the brightness of His coming. The coming of the *lawless one* is according to the working of Satan, with all power, signs, and lying wonders, and with all unrighteous deception among those who perish, because they did not receive the love of the truth, that they might be saved. And for this reason God will send them strong delusion, that they should believe the lie. [2 Thessalonians 2:3, 7-11. NKJV]

Paul said the mystery of lawlessness was present even in his day, but the final rebellion of which he spoke is rapid increase of immorality in society and the great apostasy at the end of the age when much of Christianity will fall away from the faith. The great falling away by the church began in the twentieth century and continues at an accelerating pace in the twenty first century. With the coming of the lawless one (the Antichrist), all wicked deception will descend on those who refuse to love the truth and be saved. With this refusal, God "...withdraws his grace from such sinners as are here mentioned; he gives them up to their own hearts' lusts, and leaves them to themselves..."[220] Here we have the answer as to why humanists refuse to believe what is plain truth and embrace the lie.

Dietrich Bonhoeffer called "...'the Greek spirit' or 'humanism' as 'the most severe enemy' that Christianity ever had."[221] However, the humanistic spirit is not the only enemy that will play an integral role in attacking the church at the end of the age.

Moral order of the good society led astray – the lure of pantheistic religions

Humanism has been Satan's preferred tool to destroy mankind in the West for centuries and the major force for advancing his agenda in modern times. For the last 150 years Satan has also used false religions and none are more sinister and deadly than those that teach and promote pantheism through false religions and doctrines: Eastern religions, paganism, and New Age Spirituality.

> "Pantheistic ideas—and most importantly the belief that God is equal to the universe, its physical matter, and the forces that govern it—are found in the ancient books of Hinduism, in the works of many Greek philosophers, and in later works of philosophy and religion over the centuries. Much modern New Age spirituality is pantheistic. But most Christian thinkers reject pantheism because it makes God too impersonal, doesn't allow for any difference between the creation and the creator, and doesn't seem to allow for humans to make meaningful moral choices."[222]

In 1975 Fritjof Capra published *The Tao of Physics – An Exploration of the Parallels between Modern Physics and Eastern Mysticism.*

> The most important characteristic of the Eastern world view - one could almost say the essence of it - is the awareness of the unity and mutual interrelation of all things and events, the experience of all phenomena in the world as manifestations of a *basic oneness*. All things are seen as interdependent and inseparable parts of this cosmic whole; as different manifestations of the same ultimate reality.[223]

Ten years after Capra's book, Dave Hunt and T. A. McMahon wrote *The Seduction of Christianity*. In this book the authors warned the church of a large and seductive deception known as the New Age Movement which was an extensive network of groups united to promote world unity. The coalition was centered upon religious experiences and beliefs whose roots extend back to Eastern mysticism. Three decades ago, Hunt and McMahon found that many New Age practices, beliefs, and techniques were deeply enmeshed in the church including "...psychotherapy, visualization, meditation, biofeedback, Positive Confession, Positive or Possibility Thinking, hypnosis, Holistic medicine, and a whole spectrum of self-improvement and success/motivation techniques."[224]

Regarding the assault on the church, Charles Colson wrote, "The enemy is in our midst. He has so infiltrated our camp that many simply no longer can tell the enemy from a friend, truth from heresy."[225] This was written over thirty years ago! Thirty years later, these pantheistic New Age beliefs, practices, and techniques are so entrenched in many churches that they have become virtually ubiquitous. The liberal church had been infiltrated almost a century ago. While many conservative churches may have bypassed or avoided the obvious trappings of pantheism and the various religions promoting it, many have succumbed to the essence of its much more sinister and damaging message—You are God. This is the message of humanism, and it is also the message of the New Age Movement and its parent, Eastern mysticism. This message is evident from several quotes from the writings New Age leader Neale Donald Walsch. "God is creation. You are the Creator and the Created. You are already a God. You simply do not know it. You are One with everyone and everything in the universe—including God. There is only One of Us. You and I are One."[226]

Walsch was one of the contributors to a collection of articles titled *From the Ashes: A Spiritual Response to the Attack on America* written by various "spiritual leaders" and "extraordinary citizens" to address the events of September 11, 2001. Walsch challenged his fellow contributors to preach a "new gospel" and that "We are all one" which erroneously claimed that the Bible supported this message.[227] He also wrote,

> We must challenge ourselves. We must change the beliefs upon which our behaviors are based. We must create a different reality, build a new society…We must do so with new spiritual truths. We must preach a new gospel, its healing message summarized in two sentences: We are all one. Ours is not a better way, ours is merely another way.[228]

Many religious leaders are preaching Walsch's new gospel. Some are deceived but many are unapologetic disciples of "new" spiritual truths that blatantly contradict biblical truth. The condemning evidence is revealed by their words and actions as well as their New Age associations through networks, close friendships, shared training, mutual endorsements, as well as shared pulpits, platforms, and seminars.

The pantheistic beliefs of Eastern religions and the New Age movement's emphasis on oneness perverts the meaning of relationship with God and man as it strives to eliminate distinctions between God and man, between God and His creation, and between men. The "all are one" and "you are God" mantra emaciates the meaning of truth through false assumptions of equality which are achieved by blenderizing all of creation including a transcendent God into a formless and meaningless celestial soup. Pantheism is the ultimate expression of egalitarianism's equality—All are one; therefore, you are God.

Only through the Christian worldview's focus on relationships and consequent brotherhood can man give and receive the respect that flows from his image-of-God qualities found in his human nature. These are the prerequisites for building the good society.

Part IV – Defending and Preserving the Good Society

Before defending and restoring the good society, it is important to once again explain our terms and objective. In the opening paragraphs of this book it was stated that the good society is inhabited by a people who have constructed and maintain a high degree of moral and social order founded upon and held together by the glue of eternal truths, norms, human universals, mores and traditions, distant voices of the past, and most certainly faithfulness to God and the prescriptions of the Bible. This is the Judeo-Christian worldview.

In the good society will be found a high degree of *order, justice, and freedom*. However, *order* is of first importance among the three universal components of a good society. It is an *order* that includes both the order of the soul and order of society (*moral* order and *civic* order). Moral order and civic order are complementary, intricately linked, and interdependent. Disorder of one leads to disorder of the other.

Restoring order to the soul and society rests upon the shoulders of the Church and individual Christians. In chapter 15, we begin with the responsibilities of the *individual* followed by the responsibilities of the *universal Church* which is the worldwide body of born-again believers. In chapter 16, we will deal with the second definition of *church* by which is meant various church organizations and their leadership: Christian denominations, fellowships, assemblies, congregations, parishes, and para-Christian organizations.

15

Defending the Good Society – A Time for Action by Faithful Christians

John Donne (1571-1632) wrote his famous poem which stated that "No man is an island entire of itself." Donne was a Christian, and the essence of this poem was that human beings do badly when isolated from others and must be part of community in order to survive and thrive. Donne's immortalization of this eternal truth cuts to the heart of the difference between Christianity and humanism—*God's relationship-centered biblical worldview* and man's *self-centered humanistic worldview*.

Right relationships give rise to moral and civil order which makes possible unity with God and unity in marriage, family, community, and the nation. Self-centeredness leads to loss of order in the soul and society as self is exalted above God and human relationships. So how does a one fight the forces of evil in the seemingly impossible task of restoring moral order of the soul and civic order in society?

The Individual - soldiering in defense of the good society

For the *Christian*, defending the good society means you must be fully equipped and prepared to do battle against principalities, against powers, against the rulers of the darkness of this age, against spiritual hosts of wickedness in the heavenly places. The Apostle Paul's letter to the Ephesians expands on these preparations and duties:

> Finally, my brethren, be strong in the Lord and in the power of His might. Put on the whole armor of God, that you may be able to stand against the wiles of the devil. For we do not wrestle against flesh and blood, but against principalities, against powers, against the rulers of the darkness of this age, against spiritual *hosts* of wickedness in the heavenly *places*. Therefore take up the whole armor of God, that you may be able to withstand in the evil day, and having done all, to stand. Stand therefore, having girded your waist with truth, having put on the breastplate of righteousness, and having shod your feet with the preparation of the gospel of peace; above all, taking the shield of faith with which you will be able to quench all the fiery darts of the wicked one.

And take the helmet of salvation, and the sword of the Spirit, which is the word of God; praying always with all prayer and supplication in the Spirit, being watchful to this end with all perseverance and supplication for all the saints— [Ephesians 6:10-18. NKJV]

Having been properly prepared with the full armor of God, we can stand against the wiles of Satan in that evil day, and having done all, we stand in spite of circumstances, personal sacrifices, persecution, and even death.

There are many *non-Christians* allies who wholly believe in, support, and want to preserve the good society, but without a personal relationship with God, they stand at the periphery of the battle, do not have status with the Commander, and enter the battle without the full armor of God. For the *non-Christian* allies who want to preserve the good society, their efforts begin by enlisting in God's eternal kingdom. To enlist, the non-Christian is required to establish a relationship with the God of truth, that is, become a Christian.

For some who have never known God or never understood the tenets of Christianity, becoming a Christian may seem unimportant, confusing, non-rational, and even embarrassing because they have spent their entire lives listening to humanism's incessant drumbeat which promotes the false freedom of self and denies the strictures of a supernatural God. Often, they may be discouraged because they have preconceived notions of what must occur to become a follower of Christ. Does one's enlistment require the non-Christian to follow the Apostle Paul's Roman road of scripture verses, recite certain phrases, and stand before the congregation of a local church and swear allegiance to God and his commandments forever, amen? There is nothing wrong with that if you mean it. However circuitous your path to God may be, it must always end with a one-on-one encounter between the sinner and God. To be born again means that a person has repented of his or her sin, accepted Jesus as his or her Lord and Savior, and desires to follow Him and His commandments for the remainder of his or her life. Each time a human being comes to Christ (being saved, born-again) is a unique and distinctive experience, as matchless as a single fingerprint or snowflake. The Christian's relationship with Christ is a personal, loving, one-on-one relationship and always will be.

Perhaps a brief personal example of this author's road to God will help. I became a Christian as a child of six. The little town of Owasso in northeastern Oklahoma was a farming community, a tiny little hamlet of about 250 people, barely four blocks long and two blocks wide straddling a two-lane concrete highway meandering southward towards Tulsa through the perennially-flooding bottom lands and across an old bridge over Bird Creek. This little wide spot in the road had two or three churches, a grocery store or two, a school, a collection of small houses, and not much else. Our children's church teacher and her husband (a nonbeliever) were dairy farmers as were my parents and as were my mother's parents before them. I still remember well those Sunday mornings when she taught us with flannel graph stories from the Bible including Noah, Moses, Joseph, David and Goliath, and Daniel in the lion's den. She mixed in her own stories of "Barney in the Barrel," "The Little Red Hen," and others, all reflecting the truth of Christ's sacrificial love for each of us.

One Sunday morning she asked if any of us (probably about eight or nine in attendance that morning) would like to accept Jesus into their heart. I moved from the back row of three homemade benches, came to the front, and accepted Him as my Lord and Savior. Why did I *believe?* Some will say my child's faith was mere emotional manipulation by an adult. Others will say it was the pressure of Christian family and friends to conform to the family's faith. But the Bible gives the real reason. *I believed because my child-like faith responded to the gentle wooing of the Holy Spirit.* Luke recorded Christ's words as He described the utmost importance of a child-like faith, "Assuredly, I say to you, whoever does not receive the kingdom of God as a little child will by no means enter it." [Luke 18:17. NKJV]

But the act of becoming a born-again Christian is only the beginning. One cannot stay a Private E-1 in God's kingdom forever. Just as we grow physically and mentally, our child-like faith must not remain static. Since that day when I moved from the back bench to publicly profess my faith in Jesus and accept Him as my Lord and Savior, my faith has grown and continues to grow because of *reason*.

Right reason applied to my observations and experiences in the light of the biblical revelation and divine guidance of the Holy Spirit increases my faith and helps me in my everyday life's walk of faith. Life happens, and bad things happen to people who are faithful to God. How should Christians respond when they experience the trials of life such as when a spouse unexpectedly files for divorce, the death of a child or spouse, loss of job, betrayal by friends, and agonizing pain or loss of health? These are times when right reason helps sustain faith in times of adversity. The believer continues to believe because he or she knows the truth of God's word and because their life's observations and experiences substantiate those eternal truths upon which their faith rests. All the while the world shouts that there can be no faith in a God who would allow such tragedies, but the world only sees the natural and temporal. Faith transcends the natural into the realm of the supernatural and the reality of eternity.

Faith is not an abandonment of reason. C. S. Lewis challenged the widespread assumption that there is a battle between faith and reason, "It is not reason that is taking away my faith: on the contrary, my faith is based on reason. It is my imagination and emotions [that attack faith]. The battle is between faith and reason on one side and emotion and imagination on the other."[229]

Reason is an ally of faith. Our observations and experiences of life aided by right reasoning lead us to belief in the truth of Christianity and all upon which it rests in spite of circumstances. In one sense reason leads us to the door of Christianity, but faith invites us in and holds our hand as we continue the faith journey. However, reason was not left at the door. As we move along our faith journey, we encounter life—all sorts of thoughts, ideas, things, situations, difficulties, trials, struggles, disappointments, opportunities, and so forth. At that point reason continues to assist and guide within the framework of truths we hold and have incorporated into our faith walk. In this sense, reason helps us to accept the seemingly unreasonable as we search the Bible, pray for Divine guidance, and work out our own salvation.

Lewis captures well the linkage between faith and reason when he wrote that faith "…is the art of holding on to things your reason has once accepted, in spite of your changing moods."[230] It is not a blind faith but a faith that is supported and increased through right reason. In time, faith grows to be more important to our belief in the God of the Bible than our reasoning ability. Faith never abandons reason for reason continues to play a secondary and supporting role. As faith grows and reason diminishes, we understand that reason has helped us come full circle once again to a child-like faith, and through faith we can withstand changes in our moods, our failures, our doubts, our circumstances, or any other of life's challenges. I *believed* as a child of six because of a child-like faith. I *continue to believe* and my faith grows as right reason filters my observations and experiences in life in the light of the biblical revelation and divine guidance.

I have spent considerable time in this section writing of the importance of the individual becoming a child of God. I have done so because the reader's personal salvation is more important to you and your eternal destiny than your efforts in defense of the good society. However, once enlisted, your active participation in that defense of the good society is essential for your spouse, family, community and nation in which you and generations to come will continue to live while on this earth. Once your eternal relationship with God is established, it is time to turn our attention to your relationship with the rest of humanity.

The Body of Christ - soldiering in defense of the good society

Once enlisted, individual Christians have become members of the body of Christ (the universal Church – Jesus' faithful followers worldwide) and are responsible for creating and maintaining the good society. In other words, we are individual members of His kingdom, but we are also linked with all other Christians. This linkage starts with one's inner circle, the spouse and family. We must work to win those in our family and extended family who are not faithful followers of God. Parents must teach their children and grandchildren about Christianity, the good society, and the moral and civic order upon which it sits. They must be taught that the good society is based on objective truth which is found in the nature of God and His Holy Word, the Bible. We must live exemplary lives of holiness and good works. We must support and vote for candidates for office at all levels of government and should consider seeking an office or leadership positions in the public and civic arenas. We must become leaders in our spheres of influence wherever they may be. We must expose and speak out with fervor and persistence against the destroyers of order, justice, and freedom. In effect, we must become warriors in the cause of the good society.

Although the above actions may seem insignificant in light of the enemy's overwhelming numbers and powerful forces which seemingly assure our defeat, Christians have four invaluable resources that give renewed strength, support, and encouragement when challenged by the forces of evil and when disaster appears imminent.

- God's direct intervention in human affairs for His people

The first resource that brings encouragement is the many examples of *God's intervention for His people* when they are faced with overwhelming and imminent defeat and destruction. When God miraculously intervenes or influences the affairs of men, this is called the *providence of God* by which is meant influence or intervention that is not of human origin but divine. The Old Testament is replete with numerous miraculous interventions on behalf of Israel. We need only to look to the examples: Moses freeing the people of Israel against the might of Pharaoh and the Egyptian empire, David defeating Goliath, and Gideon and his three hundred warriors. God's miraculous interventions in the affairs of nations and individual men and women continue in the modern world, perhaps even more so in these perilous last days of the end time.

- Assurance of His future and final victory in the war between good and evil

The second resource that brings encouragement is God's assurance to His people of *His future and final victory* in the global war between good and evil at the end of the age. Given the vast carnage and disorder brought about by the humanistic worldview and false religions in all facets of society, a Christian's efforts to redeem and preserve the good society and its civic order may seem as though we they are bailing water with a bucket on the sinking *Titanic*. However, Christians must remember that whether or not they win the present battle to preserve the good society in America, the faithful followers of the God of the Bible are victors at the end and will experience and participate in the perfect moral and civil order of God's kingdom at the end of the age.

- The inner presence and working of the Holy Spirit within Christians

Third, we must remember that faithful, born-again Christians have the *Holy Spirit residing within them.* The Holy Spirit is the Christian's secret weapon, and He will supernaturally encourage and guide them. He will provide the spiritual strength and provision sufficient to allow the Christian to unwaveringly stand in the hour of battle.

- God answers the Christian's prayers

Fourth, Christians must be faithful to pray for the restoration of the good society. Just one example of many of the *power of concerted prayer* by faithful Christians is found in American history during the last decade of the 1700s.

Following the American Revolution (1776-1781) and efforts to form a new nation, there was a second ebbtide of religious fervor and an increase in secularism and irreligion, especially in the decade of 1790s. America's spiritual and moral decline threatened the survival of the new republic. As a result of coordinated and concerted prayer of pastors and laity of American churches, the Second Great Awakening crossed the Atlantic in the late 1790s and resulted in a spiritual and moral regeneration and initiated other civilizing influences on the young nation. These influences included popular education, Bible Societies, Sunday schools, the modern missionary movement, and ultimately sowed and nurtured the seeds that led to the abolition of slavery.[231]

Just as the First Great Awakening was the *formative* moment in American history preceding the political drive for independence and making it possible, the Second Great Awakening was the *stabilizing* moment that saved the new nation from political and moral destruction and whose effects lasted until the 1840s.

16

The Good Society and the Organized Church[*]

Here we must distinguish between *the Church* which in the previous chapter we have described the universal church, the body of born-again followers of Jesus Christ around the world. The second definition of *church* includes various Christian organizations and their leadership: denominations, fellowships, assemblies, congregations, parishes, and para-Christian organizations. It is this second group and their leadership to which we devote our attentions in this chapter.

In the Western world particularly, it is the organized church and its leadership to which the universal church has commissioned to lead in the defense of the good society. For almost three quarters of a century, that defense by a large number of these organizations and their leadership has been abysmal and even non-existent. Christian apologist and author Os Guinness describes the result of the abdication of the organized churches' responsibility to defend the good society.

> Christians in the West are living in a grand clarifying moment. The gap between Christians and the wider culture is widening, and many formerly nominal Christians are becoming "religious nones"…
>
> We face a solemn hour for humanity at large and a momentous showdown for the Western church. At stake is the attempted completion of the centuries-long assault on the Jewish and Christian faiths and their replacement by progressive secularism as the defining faith of the West and the ideology said to be the best suited to the conditions of advanced modernity. The gathering crisis is therefore about nothing less than a struggle for the soul of the West…[232]

But the seeds of this abdication of responsibility were planted long before its tares sprang forth in recent decades. After two centuries of growth, anti-Christian progressive secularism in America has recently achieved critical mass and now boldly attacks Christians and Christianity in every sector of American society. We must ask how the church arrived

---

[*] Much of the content of this chapter comes from two articles first written and posted by the author on his website *CultureWarrior.net* during the fall of 2016: "The Church Triumphant – Parts I and II."

at this sorry state of powerlessness in defending the faith and influencing American culture.

The large and momentous showdown between the Western church and humanistic progressive secularism is also occurring during the time of the great apostasy within the church—a confluence of events in which Christianity is caught in the perfect storm. Paul spoke of the end of the last days in which much of the church would become apostate, that is, falling away from or departure from the faith.

> "Now, brethren, concerning the coming of our Lord Jesus Christ and our gathering together to Him, we ask you, not to be soon shaken in mind or troubled, either by spirit or by word or by letter, as if from us, as though the day of Christ had come. Let no one deceive you by any means; for *that Day will not come* unless the falling away comes first, and the man of sin is revealed, the son of perdition..." [2 Thessalonians 2:1-3. KJV] [emphasis in original]

Is the Christian West in that day spoken of by Paul? Considering what has happened over the last two hundred years in Europe and America, Kevin Swanson called this period "the most significant Christian apostasy of all time. As measured by sheer numbers, there is no other apostasy so extensive in recorded history."[233] Without doubt, the church is in the time of great apostasy.

An apostate church is a powerless church because it has fallen away from or rejected the truth of God's word. Over time the adulterated message of these churches becomes unrecognizable when compared with the inerrant teachings of the Bible, and without a firm foundation of biblical truth, they have become powerless.

Satan subverts the church by injecting into it the very thing in which it is in a struggle to the death—a simpering humanistic worldview that caters to self. Guinness wrote that these church leaders are "courting spiritual and institutional suicide" for themselves and for those they are leading astray. Once again Os Guinness shines light into the dark corners of a powerless church.

> ...[They] are reaping what others sowed with such fanfare a generation ago. For were we not solemnly sold a barrel of nonsense in the form of maxims that all good seeker-sensitive and audience-driven churches were to pursue? Here is one example from a well-known Christian marketing consultant: "It is also critical that we keep in mind a fundamental principle of Christian

> communication: the audience, not the message, is sovereign."
>
> The audience is sovereign? No! Let it be repeated a thousand times, *no*! When reaching out as the church of Jesus, the message of the gospel and Jesus the Lord of the message is alone sovereign—and never, never, never the audience...[234] [emphasis in original]

Church Growth leaders cry foul and say that they are only changing their methods and not their doctrine. But their methods are in truth filled with the humanistic spirit of the age that undermines or ignores doctrinal truths and are leading millions to an eternity in hell.

Seeker-sensitive churches in their quest to please the seeker have compromised the gospel and allowed the world to change the church instead of the church changing the world. Over the course of the last seventy-five years, much of the church failed to defend the faith in the public square and failed to transmit its values to its children. Many modern church leaders also have drunk deeply from the well of doctrinal heresy and have allowed the marginalization of Christianity in the larger culture. The evidence is abundant and undeniable. Many have endorsed the tenets of humanism's faith: abortion, homosexuality, relativism, higher criticism of the Bible, evolution, progressivism, multiculturalism, diversity, religious universalism, promotion of socialist-Marxist concepts of organizing society, heretical concepts of salvation, and such like. They are digging their own graves and have betrayed their God.

Hosea's description of Israel's sinful state is a harbinger of what awaits the Western church without repentance and turning back to God.

> They sow the wind, And reap the whirlwind. The stalk has no bud; It shall never produce meal. If it should produce, Aliens would swallow it up. [Hosea 8:7. NKJV]

Much of the modern church has foolishly sown to the wind and is reaping a whirlwind. Hosea's prophesy revealed sin and pronounced judgements on a people that would not be reformed and had become apostatized over several generations.[235] Our modern crisis of the soul in Western civilization has arisen because the majority of the Western Christian church is powerless to defend the faith let alone win the lost. There is little truth, little harvest, and what little harvest occurs is devoured by a cunning and rapacious humanistic secularism driven by satanic forces.

Does this mean an end to Christianity? *Never!* Whirlwinds need not be followed by obituaries. God is ready to redeem returning sinners (both individuals and nations) and restore a right relationship with Him. The true Church lives and will always remain triumphant.

So what should the faithful remnant, the universal Church, do in the face of the organized churches' betrayal of the faith and retreat from defense of the moral and civic order upon which the good society rests?

17

The Faithful Remnant must follow the Narrow Path

The leadership and most of the laity of the liberal-progressive Protestant churches since the beginning of the twentieth century and the Roman Catholic Church in more recent times have wholeheartedly embraced the spirit of the world and the dominant humanistic culture in their vigorous pursuit of cultural relevancy. As we have previously discussed, many evangelical churches have followed their example and began to march to the beat of the same drummer by accommodating the spirit of the world within their churches.

As a result of the abandonment of New Testament Christianity by many evangelicals, there is occurring in American evangelicalism a fundamental realignment among evangelicals as the various church organizations and their leadership coalesce around either a mainstream secularism or a return to evangelicalism's roots found in New Testament Christianity. This realignment will divide the evangelical church whose two branches are symbolized by the ancient churches at Laodicea (lukewarm) and Philadelphia (faithful).

Paul wrote to the Thessalonians with regard to this division in which a great number of the once faithful will renounce, desert, or become traitors to their faith (See: 2 Thessalonians 2:1-3). As previously noted, the rebellion of many in the church is called the Great Apostasy at the end of the last days of the Church Age. But Paul told us that this must come. Those that remain true to the faith should not be shaken in mind, distraught, or troubled. In the twenty-first century, this faithful remnant is the modern incarnation of New Testament Christianity. This remnant must follow two courses of action in order to preserve the faith and defend the good society.

A word to the Church – seek spiritual renewal and healing for the land

Spiritual renewal and healing for the land are modern-day synonyms for a renewed moral and civic order necessary for the preservation of the good society. We look to the Old Testament example of God dealing with King Solomon and the Israelite people and His requirements for restoring the moral and civic order of their ancient society.

> Then the LORD appeared to Solomon by night, and said to him: "I have heard your prayer, and have chosen this place for Myself as a house of sacrifice. When I shut up heaven and there is no rain, or command the locusts to devour the land, or send pestilence among My people, if My people who are called by My name will humble themselves, and pray and seek My face, and turn from their wicked ways, then I will hear from heaven, and will forgive their sin and heal their land. [2 Chronicles 7:12-14. NKJV]

In these verses God is speaking to Solomon who had built the First Temple in Jerusalem as a monument to God and as a permanent home for the Ark of the Covenant. Here, God has responded to Solomon's prayer of consecration of the Temple.

It is very important that we understand to whom God is speaking. God required *His people*, not the culture at large, to do certain things in exchange for fulfilling his promises. Some may argue that 2 Chronicles 7:14 was a promise to ancient Israel and has nothing to do with the church today. However, the verse is both descriptive of God's dealings with Israel and also prescriptive for His people through successive generations. In other words, the verse was not only a promise to Israel but a biblical principle that when followed down through history has been proven to dramatically revive the church as well as change the destiny of cultures and mankind for the better. God was talking to His people called by His name at that time in Israel, but He was also talking to His people called by His name down through the centuries to the present day.

God requires four things before a spiritual renewal and healing of the land is granted, that is, a restoration of moral and civil order. During times of spiritual and moral decline within the churches and nations, God will hear His people when four conditions listed in verse 14 are met. He will respond by fulfilling His promises of spiritual revival, renewed purpose, and restored blessings.[236] In legal parlance, these conditions and promises are the equivalent of "If...then" clauses in a legal contract or agreement: "If my people will...then I will..." The four conditions are applicable to God's people in all ages.

- Humility

The first requirement is humility. God's people must humble themselves. True humility is a brokenhearted expression of spiritual poverty and wretchedness. This humility comes from their shame and chastisement as their pride and sinful natures are exposed and for which they now express deep sorrow.

- Prayer

The second requirement is prayer, but it is a special kind of prayer. Intercessory prayer occurs when someone faithfully and continually pleads with God to take action with regard to another person, other people, or a situation. The precursor to all revivals is that one or more individuals begin to feel a growing disquiet in their souls. This may be accompanied by recognition of an unrelenting feeling of emptiness within, a deep hunger or yearning because the presence of God has departed from the midst of His people. This anguish of soul does not pass but grows into a burden that continually weighs on the hearts of one or more intercessors. In some circumstances the burden may spring suddenly from a long season of brooding discontent with the low spiritual state of the church and/or the moral and spiritual decline of a nation.

- Seek God's face

Seeking God's face is seeking his presence. When God's presence is withdrawn, Christians feel it. The individual Christian and the body of Christ must turn back to God and seek his presence once again with passion born of an all-consuming desire to feel and see more clearly the nearness of His presence. This leads to a deeper and closer relationship with Him. As the Christian basks in His presence, there will be an increasing desire to please Him by obeying His commandments, plans, and purposes for his or her life and that of the church.

- Turn from sinful ways

Christians must repent for their sins and turn from their own sinful ways and rebellion against God. This is a separation from evil influences while focusing on a life of purity and holiness. The separateness of the church from worldliness and the wicked is a consistent theme which runs throughout the Bible, particularly in the New Testament. We must contend for separateness which is the narrow path as described by Christ near the end of the Sermon on the Mount. "Enter by the narrow gate; for wide *is* the gate and broad *is* the way that leads to destruction, and there are many who go in by it. Because narrow *is* the gate and difficult *is* the way which leads to life, and there are few who find it." [Matthew 7:13-14. NKJV]

Today, much of the modern church exhibits the opposites of God's requirements for spiritual renewal and healing of their land. It is proud, prayerless, without God's presence, and sinful. The defining characteristic of the modern church is *self* or *self-centeredness* which numbs the soul to things eternal. Its polar opposite is the overarching importance of *relationship* (man to God and man to man) which is the keystone of the Christian faith. Much of the modern church is a picture of the lukewarm church at Laodicea as judged by Jesus in Revelation 3. Being spiritually lukewarm is the essence of the modern church's focus on self. It signifies contentment, lethargy, apathy and comfortable conformity. It is a dying if not dead church whose cadaver is always adjusting to the temperature of the spirit of the world around it. Thus, it is neither hot nor cold. It is the church with the Do Not Disturb sign hung on its front door, and that message is meant for both God and humanity.

The modern Laodicean church can be changed only by repentance and a spiritual revival. While many in the church are dabbling with other gospels and seeking other Jesuses just as they did in the time of the apostles, there is a faithful remnant that is seeking forgiveness for their sins, hungering for revival of the church, and a healing of their land. But God's power and presence will not return to the Church until all four of His requirements for revival are met.

Those sincerely seeking revival are compelled to pray that sin residing in the camp will be recognized, exposed, and expelled through the work of the Holy Spirit. To do so the church must have bold preachers and lay men and women full of the Holy Spirit and wisdom who have humbled themselves, are praying for revival, are seeking the face of God, and who are not afraid to confront sin and preach the uncompromised message of Jesus Christ to a hurting, lost, and hell-bound world.

A Word to the individual Christian – Stand fast!

The circumstances and events in the political, economic, and social arenas that Christians see as disastrous for the organized church and the universal Church are only passing scenes in the unfolding drama that God is directing as the end of the age approaches. Nations that turn their back on God and His laws are paying a high price for their disobedience. Although Christians are aliens in a foreign and hostile land, they are also citizens of these earthly regimes and likewise will suffer because of their nation's descent into wickedness. Even now the body of Christ (the Church) in many nations is experiencing a measure of this suffering before the rapture of the Church. But the Church must never forget that their real home is in the wonderful and eternal presence of God. His purposes for allowing these momentary afflictions are often beyond our ability to comprehend, but He has assured His followers that, "...we know that all things work together for good to those who love

God, to those who are the called according to *His* purpose." [Romans 8:28. NKJV]

In light of the seeming meltdown of organized Christianity in America and the Western world, many faithful Christians are exceedingly distraught about the future. Although Christians (the universal Church) should be greatly disturbed and dismayed at what is happening in America and throughout the world, they should never be fearful of the future and never believe that the Church has been defeated. The words of Isaiah assure God's people of His and their ultimate victory. "So shall they fear The name of the LORD from the west, And His glory from the rising of the sun; When the enemy comes in like a flood, The Spirit of the LORD will lift up a standard against him." [Isaiah 59:19. NKJV] Even when the ungodly rule the land, Daniel reminds us that God is in charge of the times and seasons and that He removes kings and sets up kings (See: Daniel 2:21). Thus we know that God is sovereign and that He orders the affairs of men in all ages and all places.

In spite of the enemy's flood of evil that is relentlessly attacking the Church and the moral and civil order of the good society, Christians must continue to have

> …hearts that can melt with compassion, but with faces like flint and backbones of steel who are unmanipulable, unbribable, undeterrable and unclubbable (not coerced through comfortable conformity) without ever losing the gentleness, the mercy, the grace and the compassion of our Lord.[237]

Therefore, in the evil day, when Satan and the world has said all and done all that it can against Christ's Church, fear not and stand fast and resist the enemy even unto death! We can do so because that itinerate preacher who trod the hills and valleys of ancient Palestine two thousand years ago really was the Son of God and His kingdom will never fail.

Addendum

(1) Differences between Christian and Humanist worldviews – a Summary

Defending the Good Society is about the cataclysmic battle between Christian and humanistic worldviews, principally in modern America. In this section we shall briefly summarize, compare, and contrast the beliefs and assumptions of each worldview with regard to God, man, government, and society.

God and Creation

In the Christian worldview, God existed before time, creation of the universe, and all therein including the earth and mankind. He stood outside the universe and created matter out of nothing.

Humanism denies the existence of a supernatural, creative force in the creation of the universe. Its gospel is naturalism which insists that the unending universe of space and time are all parts of one great Nature including the earth and human beings. Existence and Nature are the same, and apart from Nature nothing exists. An explanation of everything that exists can be obtained through observation of the forces of nature. In the naturalistic explanation, the universe is an endless and unbroken series of causes and effects through time. Humanists claim that creative matter, the stuff of the universe, does not need a Prime Mover to jump-start the universe and keep it going. On the contrary, humanists claim that the universe is auto-dynamic in its existence, development, operation, and continuation.

Man's Purpose

God created mankind for a special and mutual relationship with the Creator. God did not create man out of need. Rather, it was a will to love, an expression of the very character of God, to share the inner life of the Trinity. Therefore, in the Christian worldview, man's purpose is to glorify God, to love and be loved by Him, and to enjoy interacting with Him and His creation for eternity. Since man was created in His image, he must develop those "image of God" qualities to be in harmony with God's purpose.

In the humanist worldview, the main purpose of human life is to advance the happiness of man through the development, enjoyment, and making available to all the abundant material, cultural and spiritual goods of this natural world. To advance happiness, man must strive for joyous service for the greater good of all humanity in this natural world through reason, science, and democracy.

Man's Creation and Free Will

In the Christian worldview, man was the noblest of God's creatures and singly endowed with reason and free will. Therefore, the Creator also laid down certain laws of "human nature"; the laws of good and evil to which the Creator and His creation must conform. Unlike the rest of creation, man through his free will was allowed to choose or not choose to constrain his actions and conform to and be in obedience to the Creator's laws of human nature. Therefore, man can and will be held accountable for right and wrong behaviors.

In the humanist worldview, man and his human nature were not created by a Supreme Being but are products of evolution. Man is merely a complex animal without notions of moral responsibility. Humans and other life forms are the products of an infinitely long process of evolution that exceeds three billion years. The body was primary and basic but with its increasing complexity came development and integration of animal behavior and control. This integration culminated with Homo sapiens and the "phenomenon of the mind" or man as we know him today. Speech arose from man's social nature and developed from "…elementary movements, grunts, and cries…" Moral standards were not sent down from a divine creator but were rather a social product that evolved through human association. Sin, soul, and conscience were fantasies that have been replaced by instincts and drives that evolved through time. Man's reason is a slave to desires and passions which carries an implicit denial of free choice or free will. Slave reason only produces rationalizations for morally wrong thoughts and behavior. If one can act only upon the motivation of internal passions and desires or external forces, then reason is powerless to restrain those passions, desires, or external forces. Therefore, man does not have free choice and consequently cannot be held accountable for right or wrong behavior. There are no absolutes and therefore no restraints on passions which rule reason.

Man's Nature

In the Christian worldview, man is a fallen creature. Mankind's free will allowed man to think and act in ways that were contrary to God's plan and will for His creation. When man acted in ways contrary to God's laws (truths), such disobedience was called sin, and as a result decay and death entered into God's creation. This is called the Fall, and it affected not only man but all of God's creation. Man's fall separated him from God.

For the humanist, man is continuously perfectible, a process whereby he will become progressively better and better. Man is not fallen and does not need redemption. Humanists assert there is no limit set to the perfecting of the powers of man other than the duration of the globe upon which nature has spawned mankind.

Man's Position and Destiny

Unregenerate man is positionally separated from God because of man's inherited sinful nature. The Christian worldview holds that man is inherently fallen because of the entry of sin into the human race (original sin) and therefore is separated from God. But as God is a loving God, He created a way through His son, Jesus Christ, which allows man through an act of his free will to get out of the mess he created. This is the restoration, and therefore men and women who choose Christ foresees an eternity spent with his Creator. For those who reject God's son through their free choice, the gulf separating them from God remains un-crossable, and the emptiness and pain caused by their broken relationship and separation from their creator will torment them for eternity. Thus, Christians and certain other religions adhere to a dualistic view that the soul (will, intellect, emotions) is separate and independent from the body and that the soul survives the body's death.

In the humanist worldview, man is the evolutionary product of Nature, and his mind is inseparably joined with the functioning of his brain. There is no conscious survival after death because of the unity of body and personality (which includes every aspect of the mind). Therefore, humanists embrace the monistic theory which sees a close and fundamental connection of body and personality that results in an indissoluble unity. Implicit in this theory is that the personality, like the body, is not immortal and that man's earthly existence is all there is.

Man's Relationship to Man

In the Christian worldview, man is made for relationship which implies dwelling together. It is one of the fundamental needs of mankind. Man was made in the image of God, and the importance of human relationships is a reflection of the Trinitarian relationship. It is a picture of His fundamental being as shown by the Father-Son relationship and the relationship of Christ with the Church. The reflection of God's image in mankind's relational patterns is present in marriage, family, community, nations, and the Kingdom of God. Such patterns of relationship are based on fraternity and kinship.

The humanist views man's relationship with man through the

distorted lens of equality. This distortion arises as equality goes beyond equality of man before God (which humanism denies) and the law. It is also an equality that goes beyond equality of opportunity to equality of outcome. In the humanist view, man's relationship with man ultimately transcends gender, family, community, and national boundaries. In the words of *Humanist Manifesto II*, "What more daring goal for humankind than for each person to become, in ideal as well as practice, a citizen of a world community."[238]

Man as an Individual

Each individual was created for a personal and loving relationship with God. Because man is born with the mark of sin that was transmitted to him down through history from his first ancestor, the relationship remains broken. The Christian worldview recognizes the fallen condition of humankind and that God has provided a means whereby man can return to Him through repentance and living in a proper orientation to His laws and plan. A personal (individual) relationship with God is possible only through recognition of who God is and obedience to his precepts. That relationship is restored through the acceptance of God's son, Jesus Christ, as man's Lord and Savior.

Humanists hold that the preciousness and dignity of the individual person is a central humanist value in which individuals should be encouraged to realize their own creative talents and desires and exercise maximum individual autonomy *consonant with social responsibility*. As to the individual, humanists promise a freedom from the mores, norms, traditions, and distant voices of the past. The freedom espoused by the humanists gives unbridled control to the self and senses. However, one must read the fine print in the humanists' promises, i.e., individual autonomy must be *consonant with social responsibility*. Therefore, humanists harness an individual's dignity, worth, and freedom to the principle of the greatest-happiness-for-the greatest-number which is hitched to the humanist belief that the highest moral obligation is to humanity as a whole. The obligations of the individual are subservient to his obligations to the larger society, and those obligations are determined and defined by the humanist intellectual elite, i.e., God is replaced by man as the ultimate authority of what is equal and unequal, and right and wrong.

Societal Organization and Governments

In the Christian worldview, sustained order in society is possible only when its citizens achieve order of their individual souls within God's laws. As a man orders his individual soul in accordance with God's timeless truths, he also contributes to an orderly society that promotes harmonious relationships with nature and between individuals within that society. Society contains many elements of which government is only one. The Christian worldview sees governments as ordained by God for its own distinctive civil purposes and not for church purposes. The Church and government are separate institutions, but that does not imply a wall of separation stands between them. The Church is not removed from involvement in governmental affairs from the perspective of principle. Nevertheless, the Church cannot be involved in government on the basis of power as contrasted with Islam which makes no distinction between church and state in the exercise of its power.[239]

Humanists link organization of society to the enhancement of freedom and dignity of the individual which occurs when a "full range of individual liberties" is experienced. A fully functioning humanistic society must provide "…alternative economic systems…to increase the sum of human satisfaction through reduction of …disproportions in wealth, income, and economic growth" throughout the world. Such humanistic societal reorganization "transcends the narrow allegiances of church, state, party, class, or race in moving toward a wider vision of human potentiality."[240] For the humanist, government must ultimately and inevitably assume a socialistic form in order to deliver the promised human satisfactions and eradication of disproportionate wealth, income, and economic growth.

Religion

Religion is man's feeble efforts to cross the gulf between fallen man and God. It is endemic to all of mankind, in every age and every people group. The religious impulse exists because it is not linked to human experiment, invention, or ideologies but to the permanent things or first principles. However, apart from the truth offered by the Judeo-Christian ethic, religion remains powerless to span the gulf that was created by sin. It was the revelation, initially to the Hebrews and continued through the divinely inspired writings of the Apostles, which gave clarity and foundation to those truths that mankind had struggled to apprehend and points the way to bridge the chasm between God and man.

In the humanist worldview, religion is a human social construction. Its presence merely occurs as means to draw people together and give meaning to their lives. There is no room for supernaturalism for religion is merely a form of human experience and values. Human justice, not a dead God, gives meaning to human experiences and values. Therefore, humanists deny the dualism that divides the universe into two separate realms—the material and the spiritual.

Marriage and Family

The supreme reflection of God's image in humankind is in the marriage relationship followed by family. The roles of husband and wife and father and mother (monogamous married couple living with their children) are not societal constructs. The surface *patterns* and *functioning* of family may vary markedly in various cultures and societies down through the ages. However, the divinely ordered family *structure* is intrinsically a part of the fundamental identity of the family in every society and for all time. It is one of those universals or permanent things that are imbedded in the foundation of creation.

The humanistic worldview and its values focus on the individual person and his/her independence, freedom, self-actualization, autonomy, growth, and creativity. Hence, marriage becomes secondary to the individual and is at best a contractual arrangement devoid of the requirements of covenantal "self-giving" as it interferes with humanistic values stated above. Further, marriage is only one of several relational choices open to the individual. Marriage is not central or necessary for nurturing and the transmission of moral and cultural values to children. The pair-bonding elements of monogamy and permanency are individual decisions and not cultural universals.

(2) Humanist redefinition of words to dislodge the Judeo-Christian worldview from the central vision of American culture – a Summary

We have summarized the differences between the general beliefs of the Christian and humanist worldviews. Now we turn our attention to the means that humanists use to dislodge the Judeo-Christian worldview as the central vision of American culture—the attack on language. In the battle of worldviews, certain words have gained power to obscure and pervert truth and history through the schemes of humanist redefinition.

Truth

In the Christian worldview, the Supreme Being (God) formed the universe and God created matter out of nothing. He impressed certain principles upon that matter, from which it can never depart, and without which it would cease to be. These principles dictate rules of action and applies to animate and inanimate objects. These "laws of nature" must invariably be followed by the universe and the created matter therein. One exception was allowed as man could choose to follow or depart from those principles as they relate to human nature. Those principles are truths that are intrinsic, timeless, and are essential elements that provide a coherent and rational way to live in the world. These absolutes are called by various names: permanent things, universals, first principles, eternal truths, and norms.

The humanistic worldview regarding truth is one of cultural relativism which requires a suspension of judgment since all belief systems contain some truth within while no one belief system has all the truth. For humanists, all social constructions are culturally relative as they are shaped by class, gender, and ethnicity. Thus, there can be no universal truths because all viewpoints, lifestyles, and beliefs are equally valid. As a result, no man or group can claim to be infallible with regard to truth and virtue. Rather, truth is produced by the free give and take of competing claims and opinions—i.e., truth can be manufactured.

Freedom

Simply put, freedom means an absence of coercion and constraint, but freedom does not mean an absence of consequences. God created man with a free will, that is, God gave man a choice as to whether to follow or not follow God's laws and commandments. The consequences of disobedience to God's laws are readily evident in society, but those consequences should not be confused with coercion or lack of freedom. Man must suffer the consequences for wrong choices. Yet, man often blames God for the pain and suffering in the world. As he joins himself with his like-minded fellowmen in an organized society, they impose restrictions on themselves to make life better. It is a freedom to restrain one's self.

Freedom, under the humanists' perverted definition, unbridles the self and senses from any control except within the limitations imposed by the greater good for humanity. The humanist definition of freedom presumes to loose man from the bondage of mores, norms, traditions, and distant voices of the past. However, the humanists' definition of freedom, which co-joins the maximization of individual autonomy with the humanist-created primacy of the greatest good for the greatest number, is a false freedom. A society organized around the tenets of humanism cannot remain free as it will be pushed to one end or the other of the anarchy-totalitarian continuum of government. In reality, such humanistic concepts of freedom coerce the individual through the requirement of a general commonality of thought and action which is forced downward from the state to the individual. However, to be a good society, the central cultural vision of any society must command unity to exist and prosper in ordered harmony. Such unity must filter up from individuals, not be coerced or forced down on society. Without such unity filtering up from individuals, there can be no order to the soul or society, and without such order society deteriorates over time and eventually disintegrates.

Democracy

Democracy is a form of government by the people, rule of the majority, and a means of voting. Democracy is not a synonym for freedom. Other definitions and descriptions of democracy include a means but not an end, a means whereby a society safeguards internal peace and individual freedom, a means of conveying power (but not a source of power), and on occasion a means by which freedom is threatened.

Humanists have appropriated, redefined the term, and have used it to arbitrarily consolidate power and limit individual freedom. The humanist definition of democracy has been infused with a myriad of moral principles such as a commitment to liberty and equality, concern for the worth and dignity of the individual, an individual's right to do what he wishes and limits undue interference with his individual choice and action, opportunity for growth and personal realization, tolerance, and diversity. Each carries with it its own humanistic meaning. New rights, causes, and agendas wrapped in the humanistic apparel of false qualities and moral imperatives are given legitimacy as they are linked with democracy. Therefore, to oppose these rights, causes, and agendas is to oppose democracy. For humanists, democracy is method *and* goal, a means *and* an end. In effect, democracy has been elevated to something of value in itself. This is a perversion of the meaning of democracy and a perversion of what the Founders meant.

Equality

Here we speak of equality in light of the individual within the Christian and humanistic worldviews. The founding Americans relied on order that rested upon a respect for prescriptive rights and customs as opposed to the egalitarian notions of the French philosophers during the French Revolution. This difference was made clear by John Adams' definition of equality which strikes at the heart of what it really means—a moral and political equality only—that is, equality before God and before the law. This definition does not teach that all men are born to equal powers, mental abilities, influence in society, property, and other advantages. Rather, all men are born with equal rights before God and the law and by implication equal opportunity.

The humanistic definition of equality is clearly stated in *Humanist Manifesto II's* eleventh common principal, "The principle of moral equality must be furthered…This means equality of opportunity…" But, the meaning of "equal opportunity" is immediately and drastically corrupted to mean an equality of outcome by humanist requirements. To further clarify the intent of the signors of the *Manifesto,* the document states that, "If unable, society should provide means to satisfy their basic economic, health, and cultural needs, including whatever resources make possible, a minimum guaranteed annual income."[241]

This concept of human equality flows from the humanistic assumption of the perfectibility of man. Under this concept, what men are comes from experience. Therefore, men are equal at birth, and differences and inequalities arise due to environment. The goal of humanists is to achieve an egalitarian society through elimination of inequalities due to environment. This elimination is to be achieved through political means in which man, achieving perfect equality in their political rights, would at the same time be perfectly equalized and assimilated in their possessions, their opinions, and their passions. When humanists fail to achieve equality of outcome through political equality, the levelers demand economic democracy, a new and expanded humanist definition of equality. However, economic democracy still means an equality of condition as opposed to equality of opportunity and is to be achieved through recognition of invented or synthetic rights coupled with broad but non-specific egalitarian ideals. Society is leveled with guarantees of certain outcomes to its citizens, but political equality suffers.

Justice

Justice is variously defined as fairness, impartiality, right action, and the principle or process by which every man and woman in society are accorded the things that inherently belong to them (their lives, dignity, property, and status or station in life). Justice implies standards by which its office is administered. Those standards were built up over the centuries and crafted by adherence to unchanging universal truths, a set of norms that derive from an authority above the state and a people's culture across the whole of life. The concept of justice is a universal, a thing of permanence that transcends the whole of man's time on this planet and pertains to all cultures. Because justice has permanence or status, it acts as a measure or standard rather than a tool to achieve a social function or change.

For the humanist, man is an economic being, and the definition of justice must be bent to recognized humanist social values. Those values—liberty and opportunity, income and wealth, and the bases of self-respect—are to be distributed equally unless an unequal distribution of any or all of these values is equally advantageous to everyone. These values, and therefore justice charged with upholding these values, are a thing rationally constructed by man. For the humanist, justice is achieved when there is a "fair" measure of economic distribution. No god, no tradition, no patrimony, and no settled law need apply. Humanists have changed the definition of justice to fit their worldview, but like order and freedom, justice is not of human construction, and no amount of humanist tinkering will change the heart of man with regard to a right understanding of fairness, impartiality, and right action in a civil society.

Multiculturalism

The Judeo-Christian ethic recognizes the common origin of man as described in Genesis of the Old Testament. In the New Testament the Apostle Paul spoke to the assembled Athenians that the God of the Hebrews "…made of one blood all nations of men for to dwell on the face of the earth…"[242] Christians understand that God created all peoples, but those peoples have developed different cultures and worldviews. Christianity far exceeds humanism and most other worldviews in its adaptation to and civil respect for diverse cultures and governments. From whence does this adaptation and respect come? First, Christianity offers truth and therefore provides the answers to life's basic questions which help bring order to one's soul and ultimately order to those societies in which Christians dwell. Truth provides a measure of commonality between men, a set standard by which men may interact with one another. Truth also engenders trust as it is exhibited in the lives of people that are followers of Christ *and* followers of His example. Second, Christianity does not have a political agenda other that adherence to principle. Therefore, it enters and resides quietly in various societies—from free to totalitarian.

Humanistic multiculturalism is defined as a belief that all cultures are equally valid and valuable, and it claims that all cultures offer some truth while no one culture can claim to provide the answers to all of life's basic questions. The essence of multiculturalism is found in the denial of absolutes, one of the cardinal tenets of the humanistic faith. Without absolutes, societies descend to moral relativism, a values-free approach that makes it impossible to judge one period or era in relation to another or to say that one culture's ethic is superior to another. The multicultural movement is premised on the belief that America is too immersed in Western "Eurocentric" teachings to the detriment of other cultures. The imposition of the multicultural mindset, in the American educational system in particular, is an attempt to supplant America's white, male-dominated European history and the Judeo-Christian ethic which relies on absolutes. Challenges to multiculturalism are labeled as being opposed to freedom and paints Christianity as being repressive, bigoted, and intolerant.

Diversity

For the Christian view of diversity, the best explanation comes from Paul's letter to the Corinthians with regard to unity in the Church.

> For as the body is one and has many members, but all the members of that one body, being many, are one body, so also *is* Christ…But God composed the body, having given greater honor to that *part* which lacks it, that there should be no schism in the body, but *that* the members should have the same care for one another. And if one member suffers, all the members suffer with *it;* or if one member is honored, all the members rejoice with *it.* [1 Corinthians 12:12, 24-26 NKJV]

The Christian's focus is not on the individual's differences but upon diversity's contribution to the whole of society, and from this emphasis comes unity. Unity is made possible when each member is recognized as an indispensable contributor to the body.

Diversity shares a close kinship with humanism's multiculturalism and focuses on the differences within society and not society as a whole. With emphasis on the differences, mass culture becomes nothing more than an escalating number of subcultures within an increasingly distressed political framework that attempts to satisfy the myriad of demands of the individual subcultures. There is a loss of unity through fragmentation and ultimately a loss of a society's central cultural vision which leads to destruction and eventual disintegration. A derivative of the impulse for diversity is relativism and humanism's perverted concept of equality.

Tolerance

One definition of tolerance is "…the allowed deviation from a standard."[243] This definition implies a standard by which to measure other cultures as well as a limit to the extent to which deviation from the prevailing culture's standard will be allowed. Because there is a standard, tension arises between tolerance and exclusivity (adherence to that standard) demanded by culture. Tolerance suggests acceptance and inclusiveness while exclusivity implies segregation and denial (by which is meant segregation *between* cultures, not *within* cultures). A culture that values its central vision welcomes integration of diverse groups that share that common central vision. However, the very essence of culture requires that it discriminate against those outside its boundaries that do not share its central vision.

Regarding tolerance, Christian teaching speaks unerringly in defense of the concept of universal human rights and why each is obligated to respect the rights of others. The conflict with the humanist worldview regarding toleration arises with the humanist belief that man is a social animal, and his morality results from his innate altruism, a moral instinct of selflessness, though not equally developed in all humans.

For the humanist, the origin of man's morality evolved from his ability to connect value or benefit with behaving well toward others, but that value does not originate with the laws established by a supernatural God. The humanist solution to "chauvinistic ethnicity" and its consequent intolerance is to recognize a new inclusive ethnicity that certifies its membership in the world community. This transformation occurs through recognition that the state must be secular in nature and that there are secular concepts and methodologies that must be invented and applied in order to achieve tolerance that transcend individual cultural boundaries. An essential part of this new world morality requires adherence to humanist values beginning with recognition of universal human rights. Therefore, toleration begins with the denial of absolutes as no man or group can claim ownership of truth which is often the product of the free give and take of conflicting opinions. The humanist stance towards toleration is a reflection of moral relativism which is the antithesis of Christian belief and that of many other religions.

Pluralism

A pluralistic society is one "...in which members of diverse ethnic, racial, religious, or social groups maintain an *autonomous participation* in and development of their traditional culture or special interest *within the confines of a common civilization*."[244] [emphasis added] By its very essence, culture must discriminate against those outside its boundaries that do not share its central vision. From its beginnings America was a pluralistic society in that it did not have a politically established national religion, i.e., one state sponsored denomination or sect. Although exhibiting a form of pluralism that denied government interference with their beliefs, America exhibited an exceptionally strong religious sanction. This sanction was the "...power of Christian teaching over private conscience [that] made possible the American democratic society."[245] This was the central cultural vision upon which America was founded.

For the secular humanist, pluralism demands all religion be removed from the public square. This is a different interpretation of pluralism than held by Americans of the Revolutionary Era. Pluralism in modern America, as defined by humanists, must presuppose that there are no universals, i.e., no God, and that all cultures are equally worthy and valid. It is in this humanistic definition of pluralism that cultures are prone to failure. To attempt to meld together or co-mingle multiple cultures into one culture with *multiple centers of vision* is to create a powerless culture with little influence and place it on the road to disintegration.

In our world of progressive education, scientism, and mass media, the semanticists have captured the linguistic high ground through redefinition of key concepts. Regarding the consequences thereof, Richard Weaver cut to the heart of the matter.

> Just as soon as men begin to point out that the word is one entity and the object it represents is another, there set in a temptation to do one thing with the word and another different thing with the object it is supposed to represent; and here begins that relativism which by now is visibly affecting those institutions which depend for their very existence upon our ability to use language as a permanent binder.[246]

At the end of linguistic revisionism, cultures and their component institutions do not survive which rest on humanism's false arguments, pronouncements, definitions, and dogma. On the contrary, the long-term survival and prospering of a culture depends on its apprehension and incorporation of those things we have called eternal and unchanging truths or universals.

Notes

PART I – Equality and the Good Society

Chapter 1 – Order, Worldview, Equality, and Egalitarianism

[1] "Archimedes," *Goodreads,* https://www.goodreads.com/quotes/16830-give-me-a-place-to-stand-and-a-lever-long (accessed July 4, 2020).

[2] Russell Kirk, *The Roots of American Order*, (Washington, D.C.: Regnery Gateway, 1991), p. 6.

[3] Kirk, *Roots of American Order*, pp. 3-5.

[4] Richard M. Weaver, *Visions of Order – The Cultural Crisis of Our Time*, (Louisiana State University, 1964, republished by way of exclusive license by the Intercollegiate Studies Institute, Wilmington, Delaware 1995, 2006), pp. 10-11.

[5] Ibid., p. 12.

[6] Paul Kurtz, *Toward a New Enlightenment – The Philosophy of Paul Kurtz*, (New Brunswick, New Jersey: Transaction Publishers, 1994), p. 70.

[7] Matthew S. Santirocco, "Introduction," *Great Dialogues of Plato*, (New York: Signet Classics, 2008), p. vii.

[8] Albert M. Wolters, *Creation Regained*, 2nd Ed., (Grand Rapids, Michigan: Wm. B. Eerdmans Publishing Co., 1985, 2005), pp. 2-3.

[9] Ibid., pp. 4-6.

[10] Paul Kurtz, ed., *The Humanist Alternative: some definitions of Humanism*, (Buffalo, New York: Prometheus Books, 1973), pp. 177-178.

[11] "Egalitarianism," *Merriam Webster*, https://www.merriam-webster.com/dictionary/egalitarianism (accessed June 23, 2020).

[12] "Equality," *Merriam Webster*, https://www.merriam-webster.com/dictionary/equality (accessed June 23, 2020).

[13] "Equity," *Merriam Webster*, https://www.merriam-webster.com/dictionary/equity (accessed June 24, 2020).

Chapter 2 – A Brief History of Equality

[14] Confucius, *Analects*, 6th and 5th century B.C., quoted by Margaret Miner and Hugh Rawson, *The New International Dictionary of Quotations*, (New York: Signet Books, 2000), p. 501.

[15] Plato, Laws, 4th century B.C. quoted by Margaret Miner and Hugh Rawson, *The New International Dictionary of Quotations*, (New York: Signet Books, 2000), p. 503.

[16] T. H. Huxley, *The Coming Age of the Origin of Species, 1880*, quoted by Margaret Miner and Hugh Rawson, *The New International Dictionary of Quotations*, (New York: Signet Books, 2000), p. 502.

[17] Paul Kurtz, *Toward a New Enlightenment – The Philosophy of Paul Kurtz*, p. 70.

[18] J. M. Roberts, *The History of the World*, (New York: Oxford University Press, 2003), pp. 517-518.
[19] Kirk, *The Roots of American Order*, pp. 221-223.
[20] John Herman Randall, Jr., *The Making of the Modern Mind*, (New York: Columbia University Press, 1926, 1940), p. 111.
[21] Ibid, p. 313.
[22] Kirk, *The Roots of American Order*, pp. 285, 289-290.
[23] Randall, *The Making of the Modern Mind*, pp. 315-316.
[24] Ibid., p. 316.
[25] Kirk, *The Roots of American Order*, p. 348.
[26] Randall, *The Making of the Modern Mind*, p. 383.
[27] Roberts, *The History of the World*, p. 689-690.
[28] Diederik Aerts, et. Al., "World Views: from fragmentation to integration," *Center Leo Apostel*, Vrije Universiteit Brussels in Belgium, http://www.vub.ac.be/CLEA/pub/books/worldviewsl/ (accessed May 19, 2009).
[29] Charles Colson and Nancy Pearcey, *How Now Shall We Live?* (Wheaton, Illinois: Tyndale House Publishers, Inc., 1999), p. xiii; Johnson, *Ye shall be as gods*, p. 84.

Chapter 3– Order and the Good Society
[30] Albert M. Wolters, *Creation Regained*, pp. 71-72.
[31] Richard M. Weaver, *Ideas Have Consequences*, (Chicago, Illinois: University of Chicago Press, 1948), p. 19.
[32] William Blackstone, *Commentaries on the Laws of England*, Vol. I- Book I & II, (Philadelphia: J. B. Lippincott Company, 1910), pp25-28; Acts 17:30.
[33] Kirk, *Roots of American Order*, pp. 3-5.
[34] Weaver, *Visions of Order*, pp. 10-12, 20; Larry G. Johnson, "Sickness in the Soul of the American Republic – Part I," *culturewarrior.net*, February 21, 2014. http://www.culturewarrior.net/2014/02/21/sickness-in-the-soul-of-the-american-republic-part-i/ (accessed March 13, 2014)
[35] Weaver, *Ideas Have Consequences*, p. 35.
[36] Ibid., pp. 41-42.
[37] "egalitarian," *Webster's Seventh New Collegiate Dictionary*, (Springfield, Massachusetts: G. & C. Merriam Company, Publishers, 1963), p. 264.
[38] Weaver, *Ideas Have Consequences*, pp. 306-307.
[39] Ibid., p. 307.

Chapter 4 – Justice and the Good Society
[40] James E. Person, Jr., *Russell Kirk, A Critical Biography of a Conservative Mind*, (Lanham, Maryland: Madison Books, 1999), p. 97.
[41] Ibid., p. 97.
[42] "common law," Noah Webster, *Noah Webster's First Edition of an*

    American Dictionary of the English Language 1828, Facsimile Edition, (San Francisco, California: Foundation for American Education, 1995).
[43] Person, *Russell Kirk – A Critical Biography of a Conservative Mind*, pp. 97-98.
[44] Joseph Story, *Commentaries on the Constitution of the United States*, (Boston: Hilliard, Gray, & Co., 1833). Vol. III, p. 593.
[45] Jim Herrick, *Humanism – An Introduction*, (Amherst, New York: Prometheus Books, 2005), p. 38.
[46] Weaver, *Visions of Order*, pp. 22-23.

Chapter 5 – Freedom and the Good Society
[47] Ibid, pp. 22, 23, 25, 29.
[48] Alexis De Tocqueville, *Democracy in America*, Gerald E. Bevan, Trans., (London, England: Penguin Books, 2003), pp. 805-806, 808.
[49] F. A. Hayek, *The Road to Freedom – Text and Documents*," ed. Bruce Caldwell, (Chicago, Illinois: The University of Chicago Press, 1944, 2007), p.134.

Part II – Equality and Human Relationships

Chapter 6 – Equality and the God-Man Relationship
[50] C. S. Lewis, *Mere Christianity, The Complete C. S. Lewis Signature Classics*, (New York: Harper One, 2002), pp. 39-40.
[51] Focus on the Family, *The Truth Project*, Lesson 12, DVD Series, (Colorado Springs, Colorado: Focus on the Family, 2006).
[52] Glenn T. Stanton and Leon C. Wirth, *The Family Project*, (Coral Stream, Illinois: Tyndale House Publishers, Inc., 2014), pp. 82-83.
[53] Ibid., p. 83.
[54] Ibid., p. 82.
[55] Timothy Keller, *The Reason for God*, (New York: Dutton, 2008), pp. 214-215.
[56] Ibid., pp. 218-219.
[57] Matthew Henry, *Commentary on the Whole Bible*, (Grand Rapids, Michigan: Zondervan Publishing House, 1961), p. 1772.
[58] Roberts, *The New History of the World*, pp. 199-200.
[59] Herrick, *Humanism – An Introduction*, p. 5.
[60] Larry G. Johnson, *Ye shall be as gods – Humanism and Christianity – The Battle for Supremacy in the American Cultural Vision*, (Owasso, Oklahoma: Anvil House Publishers, 2011), p. ix.
[61] Roberts, *The New History of the World*, pp. 689-690.
[62] Randall, *The Making of the Modern Mind*, p. 382.
[63] Kirk, *The Roots of American Order*, pp. 29, 397.
[64] Charles Colson and Nancy Pearcey, *How Now Shall We Live?* p. 335.
[65] Neel Burton, M.D., "Our Hierarchy of Needs," *Psychology Today*,

May 23, 2012. http://www.psychologytoday.com/blog/hide-and-seek/201205/our-hierarchy-needs (accessed September 18, 2014).

[66] Johnson, *Ye shall be as gods –*, pp. 286-287.

Chapter 7 – Equality and Marriage-Family Relationships

[67] Stanton and Wirth, *The Family Project*, p. 171.

[68] Ibid, pp. 82-83.

[69] Ibid, p. 72.

[70] Robert H. Bork, *Slouching Towards Gomorrah*, (New York: Regan Books, 1996), pp.193-197.

[71] Ibid.

[72] Nancy Pearcey, *Total Truth – Liberating Christianity; from Its Cultural Captivity*, (Wheaton, Illinois: Crossway, 2005), pp. 342-343.

[73] Ibid., p. 343.

[74] Larry Schweikart and Michael Allen, *A Patriot's History of the United States*, (New York: Sentinel, 2004), pp. 444-445, 497-498.

[75] John Eidsmoe, *Christianity and the Constitution*, (Grand Rapids, Michigan: Baker Books, 2001), p. 407.

[76] Schweikart and Allen, p. 498.

[77] Charles Colson, *Lies that Go Unchallenged In Popular Culture*, comp. James Stuart Bell, (Wheaton, Illinois: Tyndale House Publishers, Inc., 2005), p. 73.

[78] "The Founding of NOW," National Organization of Women website. http://www.now.org/history/the_founding.html (accessed September 10, 2010).

[79] Stanton and Wirth, *The Family Project*, p. 169. Quoting: Margaret Mead, *Male and Female, A Study for the Sexes in a Changing World* (New York: William Morrow, 1949), pp. 188-189.

[80] Ibid., pp. 170-171.

[81] Wolters, *Creation Regained*, p. 96.

[82] Colson and Pearcey, *How Now Shall We Live?* pp. 324-325.

[83] Kay S. Hymowitz, *Marriage and Caste in America*, (Chicago, Illinois: Ivan R. Dee, 2006) pp. 3, 5.

[84] Linda J. Waite and Maggie Gallagher, *The Case for Marriage – Why Married People are Happier, Healthier, and Better Off Financially*, (New York: Doubleday, 2000), p. 203.

Chapter 8 – Equality and Church-State Relationships

[85] Charles Colson, *God & Government*, (Grand Rapids, Michigan: Zondervan, 2007), pp. 99, 101.

[86] Ibid., p. 102.

[87] Person, *Russell Kirk – A Critical Biography of a Conservative Mind*, p. 97.

[88] Eric Metaxas, *Bonhoeffer*, (Nashville, Tennessee: Thomas Nelson, 2010), p. 153.

[89] Ibid., pp. 152-153.

[90] Ibid., pp. 153-154.
[91] Ibid.
[92] Alvin J. Schmidt, *How Christianity Changed the World*, (Grand Rapids, Michigan: Zondervan, 2004), p. 25.
[93] Tocqueville, *Democracy in America*, pp. 343, 345.
[94] Ibid.
[95] William J. Federer, *America's God and Country*, (Coppell, Texas: Fame Publishing, Inc., 1996), p. 18.
[96] Hayek, *The Road to Serfdom*, p.76.
[97] Paul Kurtz, ed., *Humanist Manifestos I and II*, (Buffalo, New York: Prometheus Books, 1973), pp. 15-16, 19.
[98] Larry G. Johnson, "The reasons for governmental abuse of power," *culturewarrior.net*, June 21, 2013. http://www.culturewarrior.net/2013/06/21/the-reasons-for-governmental-abuse-of-power/
[99] David Barton, *Original Intent – The Courts, the Constitution, & Religion*, (Aledo, Texas: Wallbuilder Press, 2008), p. 28.
[100] John Eidsmoe, *Christianity and the Constitution-The Faith of Our Founding Fathers*, p. 393.
[101] Ibid., p. 394.
[102] Ibid., p. 390.
[103] Johnson, "The reasons for governmental abuse of power," *culturewarrior.net*.
[104] Ibid.

Chapter 9 - Equality and Man-Community Relationships

[105] Simone Weil, *The Need for Roots*, (Boston, Massachusetts: The Beacon Press, 1952), p. 43.
[106] Randall, *The Making of the Modern Mind*, pp. 315-316.
[107] Kurtz, ed., *Humanist Manifestos I and II*, p. 18.
[108] Weaver, *Ideas Have Consequences*, pp. 41-42.
[109] Wilfred McCray, "The Soul & the City," *The City*, Vol. II, No. 2, (Summer 2009), 8-9.
[110] Weaver, *Ideas Have Consequences*, pp. 41-42.
[111] Eddy, *The Kingdom of God and the American Dream*," (New York: Harper & Brothers Publishers, 1941), pp. 168-169.
[112] Ibid., pp. 168-171.
[113] Michael McClymond, ed., *Encyclopedia of Religious Revivals in America*, Vol. 1, A-Z, (Westport, Connecticut: Greenwood Press, 2007), pp. 117-118.
[114] Eddy, *The Kingdom of God and the American Dream*, pp. 177, 179-180.
[115] McClymond, *Encyclopedia of Religious Revivals in America*, pp. 120-121.
[116] Martin Luther King, Jr., *A Testament of Hope-The Essential Writings of Martin Luther King, Jr.*, ed. James Melvin Washington, (New York: Harper San Francisco, 1986), pp. 217, 289.

[117] Ibid., p. 302.
[118] Steve Gillon, *Boomer Nation*, (New York: Free Press, 2004), pp. 97-98; Johnson, *Ye shall be as gods*, p. 54.
[119] M. Stanton Evans, *The Theme is Freedom*-Religion, Politics, and The American Tradition, (Washington, D.C.: Regnery Publishing, Inc., 1994), pp. 40-42.
[120] Weaver, *Visions of Order*, p. 18.

Chapter 10 – Equality and Labor-Property Relationships
[121] Alvin J. Schmidt, *How Christianity Changed the World*," (Grand Rapids, Michigan: Zondervan, 2004), pp. 194-195.
[122] Ibid., pp. 195-196.
[123] Ibid., pp. 198-199.
[124] Weaver, *Ideas Have Consequences*, pp. 131-132.
[125] Ibid., pp. 134-135.
[126] Roberts, *History of the World*, p. 709.
[127] Ibid., pp. 704-705, 708-709, 711, 758-759.
[128] Schmidt, *How Christianity Changed the World*, pp. 132-133, 142-143.
[129] Ibid., pp. 132-133.
[130] Helen K. Hosier, *William and Catherin Booth*, (Uhrichsville, Ohio: Barbour Publishing, Inc., 1999), pp. 3, 192, 201.
[131] Roberts, *History of the World*, pp. 758-759.
[132] *Webster's Seventh New Collegiate Dictionary*, (Springfield, Massachusetts: G. & C. Merriam Company, Publishers, 1963), pp. 124, 828.
[133] Noah Webster, *American Dictionary of the English Language*, (New York: S. Converse, 1828), Republished in Facsimile Edition (San Francisco, California: Foundation for American Christian Education, 1995).
[134] Patrick Buchanan, "Is this end of the line for the welfare state?" *Tulsa World*, February 12, 2014, A-14.
[135] Wanda Carruthers, "Joe Scarborough: CBO Report Shows Obamacare 'Still Red Hot Mess'," *Newsmax.com*, February 6, 2014. http://www.newsmax.com/Newsfront/cbo-work-obamacare-disincentive/2014/02/06/id/551246#ixzz2tEpiNt4b (accessed February 13, 2014).
[136] Johnson, *Ye shall be as gods*, p. 393.
[137] Schmidt, *How Christianity Changed the World*, p. 207.
[138] Ibid., p. 205.
[139] Ibid., p. 207.
[140] Hayek, *The Road to Serfdom*, p. 174.
[141] Schmidt, *How Christianity Changed the World*, p. 206.
[142] Ibid., pp. 206-207.
[143] Travis Gettys, "Pope Francis rips capitalism and trickle-down economics to shreds in new policy statement," *The Raw Story*, November 26, 2013. http://www.rawstory.com/rs/2013/11/26/pope-

francis-rips-capitalism-and-trickle-down-economics-to-shreds-in-new-policy-statement/ (accessed 2-5-2014).

[144] Pope Francis, *Evangelii Gadium* (Joy of the Gospel), November 24, 2013. http://www.vatican.va/holy_father/francesco/apost_exhortations/documents/papa-francesco_esortazione-ap_20131124_evangelii-gaudium_en.html#Some_cultural_challenges (accessed February 5, 2014).

[145] "Liberation Theology Interview with Professor Rocco Buttiglione," *Inside the Vatican*, June/July 2013. https://insidethevatican.com/back-issues/june-july-2013/liberation-theology-interview-professor-rocco-buttiglione (accessed February 5, 2014).

[146] Schmidt, *How Christianity Changed the World*, p. 203.

[147] W. Cleon Skousen, *The 5000 Year Leap – The 28 Great Ideas That Changed the World*, (www.nccs.net: National Center for Constitutional Studies, 2006), p. 174.

[148] Ibid., p. 175.

[149] Clinton Rossiter, ed., *The Federalist Papers*, (New York: Signet Classic, 1961), pp. 212-213.

[150] Skousen, *The 5000 Year Leap – The 28 Great Ideas That Changed the World*, p. 173.

[151] Gale Encyclopedia of U.S. History, "General Welfare Clause," *Answers.com*. http://www.answers.com/topic/general-welfare-clause (accessed February 10, 2014).

[152] Skousen, *The 5000 Year Leap – The 28 Great Ideas That Changed the World*, p. 175.

[153] Ryan T. Anderson, "The Morality of Democratic Capitalism - How to Help the Poor," *The City*, Houston Baptist University, Spring 2012, p. 76. (Book review of *Wealth and Justice: The morality of Democratic Capitalism*, Peter Wehner and Arthur Brooks, AEI Press, 2 2010.)

[154] Kurtz, ed., *Humanist Manifestos I and II*, p. 20.

[155] Russell Kirk, *The Conservative Mind*, (bnpublishing.com: BN Publishing, 2008), p. 83.

Chapter 11 – Equality -- Traditional v. Progressive Education

[156] Weaver, *Visions of Order*, p. 113.

[157] Roberts, *The New History of the World*, p. 964.

[158] Eddy, *The Kingdom of God and the American Dream*, pp. 29, 77.

[159] Federer, *America's God and Country*, p. 21.

[160] Ibid., pp. 23-24.

[161] Reprint of 1777 edition of *The New England Primer* by David Barton, (Aledo, Texas: Wallbuidler Press, May 2007).

[162] John H. Westerhoff III, *McGuffey and His Readers*, (Milford, Michigan: Mott Media, 1982), pp. 14-15.

[163] Craig M. Gay, *The Way of the (Modern) World*, (Grand Rapids, Michigan: William B. Eerdmans Publishing Company, 1998), pp. 204-205.
[164] Weaver, *Visions of Order*, pp. 113-114.
[165] Robert B. Talisse, *On Dewey* (Belmont California: Wadsworth/Thompson Learning, 2000, pp. ix, 2, 4.
[166] Ibid., 5-7.
[167] Charlotte Thomson Iserbyt, *the deliberate dumbing down of america*, (Ravenna, Ohio: Conscience Press, 1999), pp. 5-6, 345.
[168] Sidney Hook, *John Dewey – His Philosophy of Education and Its Critics*, (New York: Tamiment Institute, 1959), p. 3.
[169] George M. Thomas, Lisa R. Peck, and Channin G. De Haan, "Reforming Education, Transforming Religion, 1876-1931," in *The Secular Revolution*, ed. Christian Smith, (Berkeley, California: University of California Press, 2003, pp. 375, 377, 380-381, 386-387.
[170] Hook, *John Dewey – His Philosophy of Education and Its Critics*, p. 6.
[171] Thomas, et. al., *The Secular Revolution*, p. 372.
[172] Robert J. Roth, *John Dewey and Self-realization*, (Englewood Cliffs, New Jersey: Prentice-Hall, Inc., 1962). Reprinted in 1978 by Greenwood Press, Westport, Connecticut. P. 101.
[173] Hook, *John Dewey – His Philosophy of Education and Its Critics*, p. 14.
[174] Ibid.
[175] Ibid, pp. 21-22.
[176] Roth, *John Dewey and Self-realization*, pp. 107-108.
[177] Weaver, *Visions of Order*, p. 117.
[178] Hook, *John Dewey – His Philosophy of Education and Its Critics*, 14.

Part III – The Goddess of Equality and the Destruction of the Good Society

[179] "virtue," *Webster's Seventh New Collegiate Dictionary*, p. 994.

Chapter 12 – Assault on Language and Free Speech
[180] Weaver, *Ideas Have Consequences*, p. 148.
[181] Paul Greenberg, "Don't give up on the American language," *Tulsa World*, (June 9, 2013), G-3; On-line source: Paul Greenberg, "The state of the language," JewishWorldReview.com, (June 5, 2013). http://www.jewishworldreview.com/cols/greenberg060513.php3 #.UbdQQpyi1qs (accessed June 9, 2013).
[182] V. I. Lenin, Quote, *The Great Quotations*, George Seldes, Comp., (New York: Pocket Books, 1968), p. 925.
[183] Weaver, *Ideas Have Consequences*, p. 158.
[184] George Orwell, *1984*, (New York: Signet Classics, 1950).
[185] Ibid.
[186] Hayek, *The Road to Serfdom – Text and Documents*, pp. 54-55.
[187] Ibid., pp. 171-172.

[188] Ibid., p. 174.
[189] Ibid., pp. 174-175.
[190] "Biography," *The Aleksandr Solzhenitsyn Center*, https://www.solzhenitsyncenter.org/his-life-overview/biography (accessed June 18, 2020).
[191] Solzhenitsyn, *AZ Quotes*.
[192] Erwin W. Lutzer, *When a Nation Forgets God*," (Chicago, Illinois: Moody Publishers, 2010), p. 44.
[193] Ibid., pp. 19-21.
[194] Metaxas, *Bonhoeffer*, p. 197.
[195] Lutzer, *When a Nation Forgets God*, p. 32-32.
[196] Metaxas, *Bonhoeffer*, pp. 293, 295.
[197] Ibid., p. 192.
[198] Dietrich Bonhoeffer, "Letters and Papers from Prison Quotes," *goodreads*. https://www.goodreads.com/work/quotes/1153999-widerstand-und-ergebung-briefe-und-aufzeichnungen-aus-der-haft (accessed June 29, 2018).
[199] "20 Influential Quotes by Dietrich Bonhoeffer," *Crosswalk.com*. https://www.crosswalk.com/faith/spiritual-life/inspiring-quotes/20-influential-quotes-by-dietrich-bonhoeffer.html (accessed June 29, 2018).
[200] George M. Curtis, III, and James J. Thompson, Jr., eds., *The Southern Essays of Richard M. Weaver*, (Indianapolis, Indiana: Liberty Fund, 1987), pp. 195-196.

Chapter 13 – Erosion of the Principles of American Civil Order
[201] Paul Johnson, *A History of the American People*, (New York: HarperCollins Publishers, 1997), pp. 28-29.
[202] Ibid.
[203] Ibid., p. 29.
[204] Henry Steele Commager, ed., "Mayflower Compact," *Documents of American History*, Vol. 1 to 1865, (New York, F. S. Crofts & Co., 1934), p. 15-16.
[205] Larry Schweikart and Michael Allen, *A Patriot's History of the United States*, (New York: Sentinel, 2004), pp. 27-28.
[206] Preamble, Constitution of the United States
[207] Zacharias, *Deliver Us From Evil – Restoring the Soul in a Disintegrating Culture*, (Nashville, Tennessee: Thomas Nelson, 1997), p. 24.
[208] Ibid., p. 70.
[209] Ibid., p. 105.
[210] Ibid., p. 124.
[211] This section and the next two sections (Loss of Unity and Denigration of Truth) were was originally written by the author in an article posted on CultureWarrior.net: Larry G. Johnson, "Sickness in the Soul of the American Republic – Part I," *culturewarrior.net*, February 21, 2014,

https://www.culturewarrior.net/2014/02/21/sickness-in-the-soul-of-the-american-republic-part-i/
[212] Richard M. Reinsch II, *Whitaker Chambers – The Spirit of a Counterrevolutionary*, (Wilmington, Delaware: ISI Books, 2010), p. 98.
[213] Weaver, *Visions of Order – The Cultural Crisis of Our Time*, pp. 10-12.
[214] Ibid, pp. 22-23.
[215] Federer, *America's God and Country*, p. 247.
[216] Ibid., pp. 10-11.

Chapter 14 – The Spiraling Decline of American Moral Order
[217] Noah Webster, *American Dictionary of the English Language* 1828, Facsimile Edition.
[218] Henry, *Commentary on the Whole Bible*, pp. 22, 24.
[219] Ibid., p. 25.
[220] Henry, *Commentary on the Whole Bible*, p. 1884.
[221] Metaxas, *Bonhoeffer*, p. 85.
[222] "Pantheism," *Merriam Webster*, https://www.merriam-webster.com/dictionary/pantheism (accessed July 6, 2020).
[223] Fritjof Capra, *The Tao of Physics*, quoted in *On Truth and Reality* Website.
http://www.spaceandmotion.com/Philosophy-Fritjof-Capra.htm (accessed March 27, 2015).
[224] Dave Hunt and T. A. McMahon, *The Seduction of Christianity*, (Eugene, Oregon: Harvest House Publishers, 1985), pp. 7-8.
[225] Ibid., p. 11-12.
[226] Warren Smith, *Deceived on Purpose – The New Age Implications of the Purpose Driven Church*, (Magalia, California: Mountain Stream Press, 2004), p. 16.
[227] Ibid., pp. 14-15.
[228] Ibid., p. 15.

Part IV – Defending and Preserving the Good Society

Chapter 15 – Defending the Good Society – A Time for action by faithful Christians
[229] Lewis, *Mere Christianity, The Complete C. S. Lewis Signature Classics*, p. 116.
[230] Ibid, pp. 115-117.
[231] J. Edwin Orr, "Prayer brought Revival,"
http://articles.ochristian.com/article8330.shtml (accessed November 26, 2010); Johnson, *Ye shall be as gods*, pp. 410-411.

Chapter 16 – The Good Society and the Organized Church
[232] Os Guinness, *Impossible People – Christian Courage and the Struggle for the Soul of Civilization*, (Downers Grove, Illinois: IVP

[233] Books, 2016), p. 22.
[233] Kevin Swanson, *Apostate – The Men who destroyed the Christian West*, (Parker, Colorado: Generations with Vision, 2013), p. 19.
[234] Guinness, *Impossible People – Christian Courage and the Struggle for the Soul of Civilization*, pp. 72-73.
[235] Henry, *Commentary on the Whole Bible*, p. 1105.

Chapter 17 – The Faithful Remnant must Follow the Narrow Path
[236] Stamps, Commentary, 2 Chronicles 7:14, *Fire Bible: Global Study Edition*, p. 723.
[237] Os Guinness, *Impossible People – Christian Courage and the Struggle for the Soul of Civilization*, pp. 31-32.

Addendum
[238] Kurtz, *Humanist Manifestos I and II*, p. 23.
[239] Colson and Pearcey, *How Now Shall We Live?* p. 417.
[240] Ibid., pp. 19-22.
[241] Kurtz, *Humanist Manifestos I and II*, p. 20.
[242] Acts 17:26 (KJV).
[243] "tolerance," *Webster's Seventh New Collegiate Dictionary*, (Springfield, Massachusetts: G. & C. Merriam Company, Publishers, 1963), p. 930.
[244] "pluralism," *Webster's Seventh New Collegiate Dictionary*, (Springfield, Massachusetts: G. & C. Merriam Company, Publishers, 1963), p. 653
[245] Kirk, *The Roots of American Order*, pp. 94-95.
[246] Curtis and Thompson, eds., *The Southern Essays of Richard M. Weaver*, pp. 195-196.

Selected Biblipgraghy

This bibliography is a substantial but not a complete record of all the works and sources I have consulted. It represents the substance and range of reading upon which I have formed my ideas presented in this book. My purpose was that these sources would serve as a convenience for those who wish to pursue further research and study on the concepts and ideas presented herein.

Anderson, Ryan T. "The Morality of Democratic Capitalism-How to Help the Poor." *The City*, Houston Baptist University, Spring 2012.

Barton, David. *Original Intent – The Courts, the Constitution, & Religion.* Aledo, Texas: Wallbuilder Press, 2008.

_____. Reprint of 1777 edition of *The New England Primer.* Aledo, Texas: Wallbuidler Press, May 2007.

Bible. Scripture quotations marked KJV are taken from the Holy Bible, King James Version.

Bible. Scripture quotations marked KJV are taken from the Holy Bible, King James Version. Scripture quotations taken from the New King James Version. Copyright © 1979, 1980, 1982 by Thomas Nelson, Inc. Used by permission. All rights reserved.

Blackstone, William. *Commentaries on the Laws of England,* Vol. I- Book I & II. Philadelphia: J. B. Lippincott Company, 1910.

Bork, Robert H. *Slouching Towards Gomorrah.* New York: Regan Books, 1996.

Capra, Fritjof. *The Tao of Physics.* Quoted in *On Truth and Reality* website, http://www.spaceandmotion.com/Philosophy-Fritjof-Capra.htm

Colson, Charles. *God & Government.* Grand Rapids, Michigan: Zondervan, 2007.

_____. *Lies that Go Unchallenged In Popular Culture.* Compiled by James Stuart Bell. Wheaton, Illinois: Tyndale House Publishers, Inc., 2005.

Colson, Charles, and Nancy Pearcey. *How Now Shall We Live?* Wheaton, Illinois: Tyndale House Publishers, Inc., 1999.

Commager, Henry Steele, editor. "Mayflower Compact," *Documents of American History*, Vol. 1 to 1865. New York, F. S. Crofts & Co., 1934.

Curtis III, George M., and James J. Thompson, Jr., editors. *The Southern Essays of Richard M. Weaver.* Indianapolis, Indiana: Liberty Fund, 1987.

Eddy, Sherwood. *The Kingdom of God and the American Dream.* New York: Harper & Brothers Publishers, 1941.

Eidsmoe, John. *Christianity and the Constitution.* Grand Rapids, Michigan: Baker Books, 2001.

Evans, M. Stanton. *The Theme is Freedom-Religion, Politics, and The American Tradition.* Washington, D.C.: Regnery Publishing, Inc., 1994.

Federer, William J. *America's God and Country.* Coppell, Texas: Fame Publishing, Inc., 1996.

Gay, Craig M. *The Way of the (Modern) World.* Grand Rapids, Michigan: William B. Eerdmans Publishing Company, 1998.

Gillon, Steve. *Boomer Nation.* New York: Free Press, 2004.

Guinness, Os. *Impossible People – Christian Courage and the Struggle for the Soul of Civilization.* Downers Grove, Illinois: IVP Books, 2016.

Hayek, F. A. *The Road to Freedom – Text and Documents.* Bruce Caldwell, editor. Chicago, Illinois: The University of Chicago Press, 1944, 2007.

Henry, Matthew . *Commentary on the Whole Bible.* Grand Rapids, Michigan: Zondervan Publishing House, 1961.

Herrick, Jim. *Humanism – An Introduction.* Amherst, New York: Prometheus Books, 2005.

Hook, Sidney. *John Dewey – His Philosophy of Education and Its Critics.* New York: Tamiment Institute, 1959.

Hosier, Helen K. *William and Catherin Booth.* Uhrichsville, Ohio: Barbour Publishing, Inc., 1999.

Hunt, Dave, and T. A. McMahon. *The Seduction of Christianity.*

Eugene, Oregon: Harvest House Publishers, 1985.

Hymowitz, Kay S. *Marriage and Caste in America*. Chicago, Illinois: Ivan R. Dee, 2006.

Iserbyt, Charlotte Thomson. *the deliberate dumbing down of America*. Ravenna, Ohio: Conscience Press, 1999.

Johnson, Larry G. *Culture Wars – Dispatches from the Front*, Owasso, Oklahoma: Anvil House Publishers, 2016.

_____. *Evangelical Winter – Restoring New Testament Christianity*, Owasso, Oklahoma: Anvil House Publishers, 2016.

_____. *Ye shall be as gods – Humanism and Christianity – The Battle for Supremacy in the American Cultural Vision.* Owasso, Oklahoma: Anvil House Publishers, 2011.

_____. "Sickness in the Soul of the American Republic – Part I," *culturewarrior.net*, February 21, 2014, https://www.culturewarrior.net/2014/02/21/sickness-in-the-soul-of-the-american-republic-part-i/

_____. "The Church Triumphant." *Culturewarrior.net*,
Part I, November 4, 2016,
https://www.culturewarrior.net/2016/11/04/the-church-triumphant-part-i/
Part II, November 11, 2016,
https://www.culturewarrior.net/2016/11/11/the-church-triumphant-part-ii/

_____. "The reasons for governmental abuse of power." *culturewarrior.net*, June 21, 2013.
http://www.culturewarrior.net/2013/06/21/the-reasons-for-governmental-abuse-of-power/

Johnson, Paul. *A History of the American People*. New York: HarperCollins Publishers, 1997.
Keller, Timothy. *The Reason for God*. New York: Dutton, 2008.

King, Jr., Martin Luther. *A Testament of Hope-The Essential Writings of Martin Luther King, Jr*. James Melvin Washington, editor. New York: Harper San Francisco, 1986.

Kirk, Russell Kirk. *The Conservative Mind.* bnpublishing.com: BN Publishing, 2008.

_____. *The Roots of American Order*. Washington, D.C.: Regnery Gateway, 1991.

Kurtz, Paul. editor. *Humanist Manifestos I and II.* Buffalo, New York: Prometheus Books, 1973.

_____. editor. *The Humanist Alternative: some definitions of Humanism.* Buffalo, New York: Prometheus Books, 1973.

_____. *Toward a New Enlightenment – The Philosophy of Paul Kurtz.* New Brunswick, New Jersey: Transaction Publishers, 1994.

Lewis, C. S. Lewis, *Mere Christianity, The Complete C. S. Lewis Signature Classics.* New York: Harper One, 2002.

Lutzer, Erwin W. *When a Nation Forgets God.* Chicago, Illinois: Moody Publishers, 2010.

McClymond, Michael, editor. *Encyclopedia of Religious Revivals in America*, Vol. 1, A-Z. Westport, Connecticut: Greenwood Press, 2007.

McCray, Wilfred. "The Soul & the City," *The City*, Vol. II, No. 2. Summer 2009.

Metaxas, Eric. Bonhoeffer. Nashville, Tennessee: Thomas Nelson, 2010.

Orwell, George. *1984.* New York: Signet Classics, 1950.

Pearcey, Nancy. *Total Truth – Liberating Christianity from Its Cultural Captivity.* Wheaton, Illinois: Crossway, 2005.

Person, Jr., James E. *Russell Kirk, A Critical Biography of a Conservative Mind.* Lanham, Maryland: Madison Books, 1999.

Randall, Jr. John Herman. *The Making of the Modern Mind.* New York: Columbia University Press, 1926, 1940.

Reinsch II, Richard M. *Whitaker Chambers – The Spirit of a Counterrevolutionary.* Wilmington, Delaware: ISI Books, 2010.

Roberts, J. M. *The History of the World.* New York: Oxford University Press, 2003.

Rossiter, Clinton, editor. *The Federalist Papers.* New York: Signet Classic, 1961.

Roth, Robert J. *John Dewey and Self-realization.* Englewood Cliffs, New Jersey: Prentice-Hall, Inc., 1962. Reprinted by Greenwood Press, Westport, Connecticut, 1978.

Santirocco, Matthew S. *Great Dialogues of Plato.* New York: Signet Classics, 2008.

Schmidt, Alvin J. *How Christianity Changed the World.* Grand Rapids, Michigan: Zondervan, 2004.

Schweikart, Larry and Michael Allen. *A Patriot's History of the United States.* New York: Sentinel, 2004.

Skousen, W. Cleon. *The 5000 Year Leap – The 28 Great Ideas That Changed the World.* www.nccs.net: National Center for Constitutional Studies, 2006.

Smith, Warren. *Deceived on Purpose – The New Age Implications of the Purpose Driven Church.* Magalia, California: Mountain Stream Press, 2004.

Stanton, Glenn T. and Leon C. Wirth. *The Family Project.* Coral Stream, Illinois: Tyndale House Publishers, Inc., 2014.

Story, Joseph. *Commentaries on the Constitution of the United States*, Vol. III. Boston: Hilliard, Gray, & Co., 1833.

Swanson, Kevin. *Apostate – The Men who destroyed the Christian West.* Parker, Colorado: Generations with Vision, 2013.
Thomas, George M. Lisa R. Peck, and Channin G. De Haan. "Reforming Education, Transforming Religion, 1876-1931." *The Secular Revolution.* Christian Smith, editor. Berkeley, California: University of California Press, 2003.

Tocqueville, Alexis De. *Democracy in America.* Gerald E. Bevan, Trans. London, England: Penguin Books, 2003.

Waite, Linda J. and Maggie Gallagher. *The Case for Marriage – Why Married People are Happier, Healthier, and Better Off Financially.* New York: Doubleday, 2000.

Weaver, Richard M. *Ideas Have Consequences.* Chicago, Illinois: University of Chicago Press, 1948.

_____. *Visions of Order – The Cultural Crisis of Our Time.* Louisiana State University, 1964. Republished by way of exclusive license by the Intercollegiate Studies Institute, Wilmington, Delaware, 1995, 2006.

Webster, Noah. *Dictionary of the English Language.* New York: S. Converse, 1828. Republished in Facsimile Edition. San Francisco, California: Foundation for American Christian Education, 1995.

Weil, Simone. *The Need for Roots.* Boston, Massachusetts: The Beacon Press, 1952.

Westerhoff III, John H. *McGuffey and His Readers.* Milford, Michigan: Mott Media, 1982.

Wolters, Albert M. *Creation Regained*, 2nd Ed. Grand Rapids, Michigan: Wm. B. Eerdmans Publishing Co.,1985, 2005.

Zacharias, Ravi. *Deliver Us From Evil – Restoring the Soul in a Disintegrating Culture.* Nashville, Tennessee: Thomas Nelson, 1997.

Index

A
Adams, John, 89, 92, 121, 156
Adams, Samuel, 95
Allen, Michael, 54
American Civil War, 53, 72-74, 97
American Revolution, 63, 71, 95, 116, 138
Archimedes, 7

B
Booth, William & Catherine, 83
Bork, Robert H., 52
brotherhood, 23, 70-75, 129

C
capitalism, 81-82, 84-89, 91-92
Capra, Friljof, 127
central cultural vision, 10, 22, 25, 32, 37, 46, 76-77, 86, 93-95, 97, 101, 106, 117-120, 156, 159-160
Coleridge, Samuel Taylor, 118
Colson, Charles, 18, 127
Communist Manifesto, 84, 89
Confucius, 15

D
Darwin, 67
Darwinist, 47, 53-54
Das Kapital, 87
Democracy, 31, 33, 69, 91, 97, 99-100, 150, 156-157
Dewey, John, 97-100
diversity, 76-77, 109, 141, 156, 159
Donne, John, 133

E
Eastern mysticism, 127-128
Eddy, Sherwood, 7, 72, 95
egalitarian, 9, 13, 23-24, 46-47, 65, 75, 78, 82, 91-92, 96, 106, 110, 118, 125
egalitarianism, 7, 9, 13-14, 23, 33, 35, 58-59, 70, 81-83, 100, 103, 105-106, 109, 112, 125, 128, 156-157
Encylopedie, 43

Enlightenment, 15, 17, 43-44, 69, 82-83, 91, 98, 125
equity, 13-14, 52

F
feminism, 52-53
Finney, Charles, 72
Franklin, Benjamin, 121
fraternity, 18, 23, 44, 68-72, 75, 77-78, 151
free will, 34, 42-43, 150-151, 155
Friedan, Betty, 55-56

G
Gallagher, Maggie, 58
Great Awakening – First, 138
Great Awakening – Second, 71, 138
Greenberg, Paul, 105
Guinness, Os, 139-140

H
Hamilton, Alexander, 89
Hayek, F. A., 64, 87, 107-108
Henry, Matthew, 41, 124
Herrick, Jim, 28-29
hierarchy, 22-24, 45-46, 50, 70
Hilary of Poitiers, 40
Hitler, Adolf, 61, 110
Hobbes, Thomas, 16-17
Hook, Sidney, 99-100
Humanist Manifestos I & II, 56, 64, 69, 75, 91, 152, 157
Hunt, Dave, 127
Huxley, T. H., 15
Hymowitz, Kay S., 57-58

I
Industrial Revolution, 53, 83

J
Johnson, Paul, 115
Johnson, William, 66

K
Keller, Timothy, 40, 51
King, Jr., Martin Luther, 73

Kirk, Russell, 7, 16, 27
Kurtz, Paul, 11, 15

L
legal positivism, 66-67
Lenin, V. I., 105
Lewis, C. S., 37, 135
Liberation Theology, 88-89
Lincoln, Abraham, 90, 97
Locke, John, 16-17

M
Madison, James, 28, 89-90
Marx, Karl, 84, 87-89, 141
Maslow, Abraham, 45-46
Mayflower Compact, 116
McGuffey's Reader, 96
McMahon, T. A., 127
Mead, Margaret, 56-57
Muller, George, 83
multiculturalism, 76-77, 108, 141, 158-159
Murdock, George Peter, 56-57

N
National Organization of Women (NOW), 55
New Age Spirituality, 127
New England Primer, 96
Niemöller, Martin, 109-110

O
Occupy Wall Street, 91
Orwell, George, 106-108

P
pantheism, 37, 127-128
Pearcey, Nancy, 18, 53
perichoresis, 40
Pilgrims, 6, 9, 95, 115-116
Plato, 11, 15
pluralism, 160-161
Pope Francis, 87, 89
Pope John Paul II, 87-88
privatization, 117-118

progressive education, 95-101, 112, 161
Protagoras, 42
Puritans, 6, 15

R
racial harmony, 74-75
Randall, John Herman, 17, 44
Rawls, John, 28-29
Renaissance, 16, 125
Revival of 1857-1858, 72
Roberts, J. N., 41, 94

S
Salvation Army, 83
Schweikart, Larry, 54
scientism, 48. 112. 161
Secularism, 17, 51, 138-141, 143
seeker-sensitive, 140-141
Shaftesbury, Lord, 83
slavery, 71-73, 138
socialism, 24, 34, 47, 81-89, 91, 106-108, 112
Solzhenitsyn, Alexandr, 109-110, 112
Spurgeon, Charles, 83
Story, Joseph, 28, 66
Swanson, Kevin, 140

T
Tocqueville, Alexis de, 33, 62-63
tolerance, 76-77, 109, 156, 159-160
totalitarianism, 107
Tragic Era, 72-73
Trinity, 39-40, 50, 149

V
virtue, 103, 116, 123

W
Walsch, Neale Donald, 128
Weaver, Richard M., 8, 21-23, 31, 70, 81, 105-106, 108, 112, 161
Webster, Noah, 28, 84, 123
Weil, Simone, 69, 75
Western civilization, 10, 22, 37,
    80-83, 85, 107-108, 117, 119, 125, 141

Wilberforce, William, 83
Wilson, Woodrow, 67
Wolters, Albert M., 21
World War II, 55, 61, 73, 87, 109

www.ingramcontent.com/pod-product-compliance
Lightning Source LLC
LaVergne TN
LVHW051556070426
835507LV00021B/2603